THE
STRATEGIC
LEADER'S
MINDSET

THE STRATEGIC LEADER'S MINDSET

UNLOCKING THE KEYS TO SUCCESS

Janet L. Polach, Ph.D.

First edition – 2024 – Printed in the United States

ISBN: 979-8-9867274-4-8

Illustrations by Nataliia Kokhanchyk. Book cover and interior designed by Sue Luehring (sjldesign.carbonmade.com).

PRAISE FOR THE
STRATEGIC LEADER'S MINDSET

"An indispensable and transformative resource for senior leaders. Readers will discover powerful strategies to revolutionize and elevate their strategic leadership mindset."

—Kris Tucker, Senior Vice President, Global Regulatory Affairs, Bausch + Lomb

"I have had the immense privilege of working with Janet Polach ("Coach Janet") for several years. Her no-nonsense insights, poignant questions, and practical tips have profoundly impacted me both personally and professionally. Now, she has brilliantly encapsulated these invaluable insights and tips into her latest book. An absolute must-read!"

— Robert J. Ehren, Senior Vice President, Securian Financial Group

CONTENTS

ABOUT JANET L. POLACH

After 20 transformative years as a U.S. Marine Corps officer and executive coach, I discovered a profound truth: leadership is not innate but cultivated. As a seasoned expert in developing leaders, I coach individuals at every level—whether they're new managers finding their footing or executives seeking greater heights—through tailored one-on-one coaching, dynamic group sessions, and immersive leadership programs.

Often, I witness vice presidents grappling with the leap to strategic thinking. In The Strategic Leader's Mindset, I unveil the seven critical mindset shifts that transform tactical proficiency into strategic mastery. This is more than a guide; it's a strategic playbook for leaders eager to redefine their impact and drive their organizations to new horizons.

Janet can be reached at:
janet@janetpolach.com or janetpolach.com

DEDICATION

To an executive leader, may this book fuel your ambition and sharpen your strategic perspective. Embrace the journey, challenge the status quo, and inspire those around you. The world needs your vision and resilience.

CHAPTER 1:

The Strategic Mindset, A Definition

Effective strategic leaders develop over time. They built their reputations by getting things done , yet they know when to let go of the day-to-day supervision, create new behaviors and habits that promote long-term orientation and cross-enterprise success. They are individuals who possess a steadfast commitment to work with and through others to achieve a vision they set, communicate, and measure progress against.

Strategic leaders lead other leaders or managers, who in turn lead teams of individual contributors. Ram Charan et al.[1] introduced us to this concept in 2011 through their seminal book, *The Leadership Pipeline*. They described the six leadership passages leaders experience as they move to ever-increasing senior roles, from managing self to leading the enterprise.. They described the difficulties and struggles each level of leader faces in taking on new and unusual challenges while letting go of previously honed skills, priorities, and values that made them successful at the last level. .

I wrote my book, *The 7 Mistakes New Managers Make: How to Avoid Them and Thrive*, to help people leaders thrive. The US invests over $1 billion annually in leadership development and coaching[2], yet only a small percentage supports individuals who are brand new to people leadership. Managers are often promoted because they are highly capable individual contributors. Yet, the skills needed to be a great individual contributor overlap only 30 to 40% with the skills required to be a great frontline manager. The challenge is even more profound when great managers, those who plan and execute well, are promoted to senior or strategic leaders.

In this book, we focus primarily on directors and vice presidents within both for-profit and non-profit organizations. These roles are expected to make a cross-organizational impact by working through multiple others rather than simply managing their own teams.

As I write this chapter, I'm reminded of Sam, an exceptional manager who was promoted to a strategic leadership role in her small manufacturing firm in Wisconsin. The CEO had encouraged her for some time to engage in longer-term, strategic considerations for the business. Yet, she struggled to find time for this necessary thinking outside of nights or weekends. Sam was a detailed problem solver. Her natural inclination was to, along with others, dig into and address the issue. However, in her new role, she discovered that this was time-consuming and that her involvement wasn't always necessary. Over several months, she learned to be more mindful of where she spent her time. She delegated leadership of the "leads generation meeting" to a direct report and then asked for an update after each meeting. By doing so, , colleagues began approaching her manager with questions, freeing her from tedious, time-consuming inquiries, which, while important, occupied much of her time.

She also developed a habit of regularly scrutinizing her calendar. She realized that many of the meetings she attended were unnecessary, as two or three of her staff members were also present. She used the extra time to reflect on long-term possibilities, improved organizational structures, and the capabilities needed to achieve them.

We will focus on how strategic leaders do fundamentally different work, which requires them to set aside many of the skills that made them successful as managers. Yes, it requires an activity pivot, but more importantly, it requires a mindset pivot. That's the challenge! Strategic leaders are asked not only to act differently but to think more strategically and decisively, focusing on the long-term instead of the immediate. We will discuss setting aside and acquiring, letting go of many of the skills that made you successful as a manager, and developing the broader organizational mindsets needed to operate at higher levels in the organization. It's not just about skills or competencies; it's about a mindset change.

THE ROAD TO STRATEGIC MINDSET

We've all seen it: industries fall into the same trap when searching for highly effective strategic leaders as they do when promoting people from senior contributors to managers. We reward highly successful managers by promoting them to senior leaders, assuming "what got them here will get them there." Yet, we expect our strategic leaders to move far beyond managing people and simply getting things done. Instead, we expect them to:

- Influence peers to champion ideas and create cross-organizational success.

- Foster team development with their managers, ensuring teams continuously broaden their skills.

- Identify organizational headwinds, both internal and external, and devise mitigation strategies.

- Use informed judgment to champion new initiatives and retire outdated ones alongside other leaders.

♟ Keep abreast of industry trends that could impact the business and develop effective responses to address headwinds.

♟ Take decisive actions on key issues to drive the organization forward.

♟ Take a position on, and work toward, the future state of the market and the organization's capabilities.

The incredible challenge for new strategic leaders is this: they are promoted to strategic roles for being terrific executors. They planned, staffed, implemented, communicated regularly, and developed their team members. These are highly valued skills for managers across industries. While these capabilities earned them promotions, they are not the skills and abilities that will ensure success as a strategic leader.

I shared some of my Marine Corps leadership experiences in *The 7 Mistakes New Managers Make*. As a retired Marine Corps lieutenant colonel, I transitioned from a frontline manager as a lieutenant and captain to a strategic leader. I learned that colonels perform different work than lieutenants and captains. That's how it's supposed to work. The Marine Corps, one of the best training organizations I've encountered, invests in its leaders throughout their careers: The Basic School for new lieutenants, mid-career schools for captains and majors, and the Army War College for colonels. These schools, often months-long, focus on the specific work required at each rank. However, most organizations lack the budgets or time to send all their frontline managers through development programs, and they often don't provide in-depth development for strategic leaders either. So strategic leaders in both for-profit and non-profit organizations are often left to figure it out on their own. This book aims to help you, the strategic leader, successfully transition by shifting your mindset in a few critical areas.

FINANCIAL IMPACT OF A STRATEGIC MINDSET

Developing the mindset of a strategic leader is not just a nice-to-have; it's crucial. The financial impact of managers failing to transition successfully to strategic leader can be significant. When managers fail to develop the skills and mindset required for strategic leadership, it can result in missed opportunities, ineffective decision-making, and misalignment with organizational goals and objectives. This leads to decreased productivity, reduced innovation, and, ultimately, financial losses for the company. Consider the following:

- Deloitte discovered that 86% of executives rated leadership as one of their most critical challenges, while 50% believed their organizations were not prepared to meet current leadership needs.[3]

- Towers Perrin found that companies with low levels of employee engagement experienced a 33% annual decline in operating income and an 11% annual decline in earnings growth.[4]

- Poor leadership practices cause many organizations to experience a 5-10% drop in productivity.[5]

- Kamal Dutta reported that ineffective leadership can reduce a firm's turnover by up to 7% and limit revenue growth by as much as 4%. Suboptimal leadership practices can cost the average organization up to 7% of its total annual sales.[6]

- The gap between the value of a company with strong leadership and one with weaker leadership can exceed 35%.[7]

- Jack Zenger noted, "Good leaders create more economic value than poor leaders, and extraordinary leaders create far more value than good ones."[8]

Wow! These numbers are staggering. While the impact will vary depending on the organization's size, industry, and history, ineffective strategic leadership can severely drain resources. You know who we're talking about: the brilliant supply chain director who reached out to a myriad of sources, bartering to enable parts to flow through the production line throughout COVID, and then promoted to senior vice president over product development and distribution. He fails miserably. He continues to focus on the comfort of moving parts from point A to B, failing to focus on the future by planning for the next global disruption from an unanticipated source.

COMPETENCY COMPARISON

As leaders progress in the organization, their work changes, and so do the skills and capabilities they must demonstrate. This requires strategic leaders to develop broader, enterprise-focused skills while setting aside some practices that served them well earlier in their management career. Consider the model below, adapted from the work of Bob Eichinger and Roger Pearlman, who years earlier created the Lominger Competency Model, which is a model I helped deploy at a major corporation.9 Once implemented, this competency model supported career development, selection, and succession planning. Because decision makers were using the same competencies to discuss different levels of employees, they were able to compare apples with apples in their talent decisions specifically.

Relating to People	Managing People	Leading People
Managing Conflict	Managing Conflict	Conflict Management
Communicating with Others	Communicating Effectively	Reading Individuals
Collaborating	Collaborating	Interpersonal Agility
Serving Customers	Being Customer Focused	Organizational Agility
Understanding the Enterprise	Developing Others	Developing Others
Building Relationships	Creating High Performance Teams	Managing Teams
Influencing Others	Managing Individuals Differently	Engagement Management
Providing Support	Cultivating Team Engagement	Project Management
		Motivating/ Influencing
		Practicing Delegation

What's important is that some capabilities or competencies remain essential throughout your career, even as you advance up the leadership ladder. Notice how some competencies are required at all levels. As you compare the competencies of individual contributors to those of leaders, some diminish, while others must be developed as one moves to increasingly complex roles.

MINDSET CHANGES REQUIRED OF STRATEGIC LEADERS

The leadership capabilities required you need as a strategic leaders are not universal. These broader competencies depend on the industry, geography, and functional focus of your organization. Yet, in my 20+ years of working with executive leaders, I have observed that strategic leaders consistently face universal challenges in senior roles. Consequently, their mindsets—the way they think about their work—must evolve. My experience and the data suggest that they include:

Think strategically. Strategic actions involve thinking and planning for the organization's long-term success. It involves making decisions and setting directions that align with the organization's goals while considering the external environment, potential opportunities, and roadblocks. It requires moving from focusing on the "here and now" to looking beyond the horizon. Acting strategically requires a holistic approach considering broader contexts, market trends, competitor analysis, customer needs, and internal capabilities. Managers typically focus on operational efficiency and delivering results within their areas of responsibility. Strategic leaders, on the other hand, must shift their focus toward broader strategic objectives, setting direction for entire functions or even the organization. While operational excellence is still important, it must be balanced with a strategic mindset.

Imagine a vice president of sales who is falling short of quarterly targets. It's not uncommon for a sales organization to offer discounts or allow customers to "buy now, pay later."

While these tactics may meet the immediate quarterly expectations, they often create larger problems for the following quarter. A strategic leader will anticipate these shortfalls early in the quarter, pinpoint where sales are falling short, and develop longer-term solutions by engaging internal stakeholders, such as marketing and production and external customers to create consistent, dependable revenue streams.

New senior executives struggle with making time to think strategically before acting, yet this is one of the most significant mindset shifts they must make. They are often more comfortable with and have been rewarded for tasks like creating reports, delivering presentations, and improving efficiency. While these capabilities are important for all leaders, strategic leaders must develop the habit of acting for the broader good of the organization, not just their own.

Empower managers. Fundamentally, strategic leaders must allow their managers actually to manage. To do this, strategic leaders must set clear expectations, meet regularly with their managers, and listen to their ideas for improving processes, systems, and teams. They must adopt the mindset that their way is not the only way to get things done.

Yet, allowing managers to manage runs into numerous pitfalls for the strategic leader. Leaders may struggle with trusting their managers to take on more responsibilities and make decisions independently. Some leaders feel compelled to maintain control, making it difficult to delegate authority. Organizational culture can also pose challenges to empowering managers. In hierarchical or change-resistant cultures, leaders may encounter resistance when trying to empower managers and decentralize decision-making. Finally, leaders often become preoccupied with their own responsibilities, making it difficult to find the time to empower and support their managers fully.. Effective time management and prioritization are essential to ensure leaders dedicate sufficient time to empowering their managers.

Overcoming these challenges requires a mindset shift, where leaders understand the importance of empowerment, communicate effectively, build trust, provide training and support, and align the organizational culture with the goals of empowered managers.

Listen more than talk. It's just that simple: prioritize listening over talking. Direct report managers and their teams are much closer to the day-to-day workings of the functions. Yet, it's common for strategic leaders to dominate problem-solving meetings, leaving others wondering, "Why are we here?"

It's not uncommon for highly effective strategic leaders to transition from one function to another. While this brings diverse perspectives to the new function, the strategic leader may lack the necessary expertise in every issue encountered. Expertise in the area is less important than strong problem-solving and listening skills. "Speaking with authority" on topics you're not familiar with can damage your reputation and that of others around you.

We will explore how leaders can shift their mindset by deepening their curiosity. We will discuss how to ask great questions and spur insights or think about things in different ways. We will also review ways to enhance your listening capabilities in a world where not listening can still appear effective.

Take decisive people actions. Every leader encounters underperformers, but not all need to be exited from their job or the organization. When debriefing strategic leaders about a difficult performance issue that was eventually resolved, I often hear, "I wish I had acted sooner." This happens, I believe, because of a leader's humanity.

Coaching can be an effective tool for these underperformers.

A meta-analysis conducted by Theeboom et al.[13] and Jones et al.[14] reviewed over 32 coaching studies and discovered that coaching has significant positive effects on performance and skills, well-being, coping, work attitudes, and goal-directed self-regulation. Yet, I've found that leaders are generally un-interested in making a significant investment in coaching for a low performer. However, I have also found by working with many coachees that coaching can turn around performance.

Taking decisive action on people issues requires a mindset shift for strategic leaders. They must evaluate the individu-al's performance, dig into their past performance, provide coaching or development, if available, and then act decisive-ly, sometimes in as little as 60 days. After all, low performers are known by others as well. Addressing performance issues early and decisively demonstrates that strategic leaders are willing to make tough decisions for the benefit of the entire organization.

Outward focus. This mindset is commonly referred to as systems thinking; it requires the leader to understand the interconnections and relationships between various elements within a complex system, often spanning multiple depart-ments. It requires you to drive the whole while keeping apprised of the parts to create solutions that serve not just one's own needs or outcomes but those of adjacent or downstream/upstream functions, as well. Take the sales loading example above. Should the strategic leader be content to exercise this strategy as a regular practice, production would eventu-ally be out of sync with their own expectations, as would the supply chain.

An outward focus demands strong collaboration with peers. This is often new territory for strategic leaders, requiring them to collaborate rather than compete for scarce people re-sources or investment dollars. Working with peers who were former competitors can be challenging, especially if you haven't laid the groundwork before, and you need to leverage these relationships. Peers can be critical and may not always collaborate beyond a superficial level. Several studies have discovered that peer scores on 360 assessments are usually lower than boss or direct reports. Atwater and Waldman[10], Bracken et al.[11], and Van Den Berg et al.[12] found that peer ratings tend to be lower compared to ratings from other sources, such as supervisors and subordinates. As a strategic leader, you must proactively build these relationships before they are needed, understanding what others do and how their teams are affected by change or recommendations. Said another way, to move the organization forward, leaders must be aligned. If they are not aligned, teams will see it and become unclear on priorities and desired outcomes. This impacts morale, speed, customer outcomes, etc.

An outward focus also involves developing relationships beyond the organization. Being involved in industry trade groups, being a member of local non-profit boards, and participating in the local community allows them to not only broaden their professional network but also give back to their industry and community.

Act courageously. Adam Grant describes acting courageously as the willingness to act despite fear and doubt, driven by a sense of moral conviction and a desire to make a positive impact. Malcolm Gladwell encourages leaders to act with courage by challenging conventional wisdom and provide an alternative way forward. Maya Angelou spoke about courage as the ability to confront and overcome fear. Aristotle described it as a virtue and emphasized the importance of facing fear and acting in the face of danger or adversity. In summary, acting courageously is a mindset to willingly act despite fear, uncertainty, and risk.

In the fast-paced and ever-changing business landscape that strategic leaders live in every day, they must be willing to embrace change, take calculated risks, and adjust their strategies when needed. Everything is unclear in this dynamic global economy. Results are uncertain; strategies to undertake them are less clear. The key is not to drive ambiguity out but to become more comfortable working with what you have and acting.

Embrace ambiguity. Ambiguity is often about risk-taking. What risk or decision are you willing to make, given what you don't know? I've worked with countless executives over the years who think they are risk takers but fundamentally are risk averse because they don't want to be burned by making a mistake. This usually sounds something like, "I'm comfortable with risk; I just need to know the most likely outcome." This personal commitment to *knowing* the outcome is the antithesis of risk-taking and comfort with ambiguity. While risk-taking is scary, the mindset must be that you're not alone; you have the organization and years of experience on your side.

Highly effective strategic leaders excel in ambiguity by shifting their mindset away from the need to clarify every unknown.

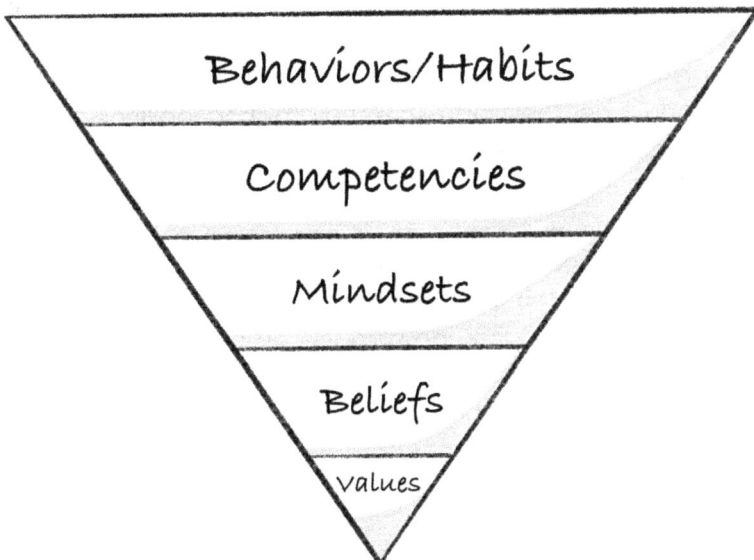

They understand risk, welcome creativity in solution-finding, and are willing to try innovative ideas that may not have been proven successful in the past. Micheal Gelb explored developing comfort with ambiguity by seeing through the eyes of Leonardo da Vinci. He emphasizes the importance of embracing ambiguity and uncertainty to foster creativity and innovation. Gelb suggests that individuals can develop their ability to navigate ambiguity through curiosity, flexibility, and a willingness to explore multiple perspectives.[15] In short, the middle name of a strategic leader is ambiguity.

SHIFTING YOUR MINDSET? READ ON.

A mindset is a set of beliefs, attitudes, and assumptions that shape how we perceive the world, approach challenges, and make decisions. It is the underlying way of thinking that influences behavior, reactions, and responses to different situations. The popular press extensively talks about mindsets as either fixed or growth-oriented, impacting how leaders view their abilities, handle setbacks, and embrace learning opportunities. Competencies, by contrast, are specific skills, knowledge, or capabilities that enable us to perform tasks effectively and achieve desired outcomes. Competencies are measurable and can be developed through training, practice, and experience. They represent the practical abilities and expertise applied in action that allow us to excel in a particular role or field.

The key difference between a mindset and competencies lies in their nature and scope. While a mindset reflects one's fundamental approach to life and work, a competency focuses on the specific skills and capabilities needed to succeed in a given context. Mindsets influence how we perceive and respond to challenges, while competencies determine our ability to perform tasks, solve problems, and achieve goals effectively.

As a strategic leader, you must evolve your mindset, often challenging the underlying belief system that has served you well up to this point.

We do this by leveraging some competencies, developing new ones, and letting go of others. Both mindsets and competencies play essential roles in our strategic success, while mindsets influence our overall outlook, competencies drive performance and results. Consider Joshua, a newly promoted executive I coached. As he began understanding "what makes this role tick," he struggled with letting go of some of the things he did so well as a director, project planning, offering team members stretch assignments. He discovered he needed to adopt a broader mindset that would ensure all projects were in sync and that all employees in his group were given the opportunity to learn and grow, not just a few high potentials.

This book shares insights on mindset shifts from many leaders I've encountered throughout my leadership career and offers ways for you to develop them. I offer various tools to use to incorporate these mindset shifts into your daily habits. In each chapter, we will:

♟ Explore the mindset shift and challenges to evolving it,

♟ Discuss the behaviors required to implement the shift,

♟ Identify what gets in the way of making the shift,

♟ Describe the benefits of overcoming these challenges, and

♟ Articulate the actions or habits needed to sustain the shift.

It's important to note that mindset shifts require continuous effort and self-reflection. Don't expect to master these shifts immediately; instead, find suggestions you can incorporate into your routine. As the business landscape evolves, strategic leaders must adopt and adapt to new mindsets to remain effective.

What is Your Strategic Mindset? As you prepare to become a strategic leader, take a moment to assess your own mindsets. How often do you demonstrate each of these habits?

	Rarely	Sometimes	Always
Think strategically. Orienting on long-term success, setting direction, making time for "thinking" and not just "doing," focusing (and acting) beyond the here and now.			
Empower managers. Allow managers to lead, lean into empowerment, create two-way communication channels to ensure initiatives are on track, guide but not take over.			
Listen more than talk. Allow others to discuss issues while being open to possibilities freely, demonstrate curiosity, and ask great questions that spur insights.			
Take decisive people actions. Evaluate underperformers quickly and equitably, consider an employee's history and future potential, and act within 60 days.			
Outward focus. Consider the whole system and not just a sum of the parts, collaborate with leaders inside and outside the organization, and give back to your community.			

	Rarely	Sometimes	Always
Act courageously. Demonstrate a willingness to act despite fear and doubt with a desire to make a positive impact, embrace change, and adjust strategies when needed.			
Embrace ambiguity. Be curious, wonder about possibilities, identify the unknowns, act without all the facts.			

In wrapping up this first chapter, I offer the following poem about managers transitioning to strategic leaders. Thank you, Chat GPT:

In a world of change, challenges unfold,
Transitions embrace, like stories untold.
From a student to a leader, in the blink of an
eye, A journey of growth, reaching for the sky.

Responsibilities rise, like a mountain so high,
Guided by others, under a watchful eye.
Yet doubts may arise, like whispers in the breeze,
Uncertainty lingers, like leaves on the trees.

But fear not, dear leader, for strength lies within,
Seek guidance and knowledge, let wisdom begin.
Embrace the unknown with an open heart,
For every challenge lies a chance to depart.

With time and support, you'll find your own way,
Overcoming obstacles, day by day.
In this transition, your spirit will soar.
A strategic leader you'd become, forevermore.[16]

REFERENCES

1. Charan, R., Drotter, S., & Noel, J., (2011). The leadership pipeline: How to build the leadership powered company. Jossy-Bass, San Francisco, CA.

2. International Coach Federation. (2020). 2020 ICF Global Coaching Study. extension://efaidnbmnnnibpcajpcglclefindmkaj/https://coachfederation.org/app/uploads/2020/09/ FINAL_ICF_GCS2020_ExecutiveSummary.pdf.

3. Deloitte University Press (2015). Global human capital trends. https://www.deloitte.com/content/dam/assets-shared/legacy/docs/industry/technology-mediatelecommunications/2022/DUP_GlobalHumanCapitalTrends2015.pdf;.

4. Schwartz, T., (2010, June). The productivity paradox: How Sony Pictures gets more out of people by demanding less. Harvard Business Review, 64-69. https://hbr.org/2010/06/the-productivityparadox-how-sony-pictures-gets-more-out-of-people-by-demanding-less.

5. GBS Corporate Training. (2017, July 13). Can you really afford it? https://www.gbscorporate.com/blog/the-cost-of-poor-leadership-on-your-revenue-and-culture

6. Spence, J. (n.d.) The high cost of poor leadership. Johnsmith.com. https://johnspence.com/high-costpoor-leadership/;

7. Deloitte, (2012, March.) The leadership premium: How companies with the confidence of investors. chrome-extension://efaidnbmnnnibpcajpcglclefindmkaj/https://www2.deloitte.com/content/dam/Deloitte/g lobal/Documents/HumanCapital/dttl-hc-leadershippremium-8092013.pdf

8. Zenger, J., (2015, Jan. 15). Great leaders can double profits, research shows. Forbes. https://www.forbes.com/sites/jackzenger/2015/01/15/great-leaders-can-double-profits-researchshows/?sh=5eo5b7866ca6

9. Talentellignet. (2024). http://www.talenttelligent.com

10. Atwater, L. E., & Waldman, D. A. (1998). The role of peer feedback in enhancing leadership: An examination of multisource feedback. The Leadership Quarterly, 9(4), 427-448.

11. Bracken, D. W., Timmreck, C. W., Fleenor, J. W., & Summers, L. (2001). 360-degree feedback: A review and an evaluation framework. Human Resource Management, 40(3), 173-192.

12. Van Den Berg, I., Admiraal, W., & Pilot, A. (2006). The relationship between peer evaluations and student performance in a college setting. Studies in Higher Education, 31(3), 341-356.

13. Theeboom, T., Beersma, B., & Van Vianen, A. E. (2014). Does coaching work? A meta-analysis on the effects of coaching on individual level outcomes in an organizational context. The Journal of Positive Psychology, 9(1), 1-18

14. Jones, R. J., Woods, S. A., & Guillaume, Y. R. (2016). The effectiveness of workplace coaching: A metanalysis of learning and performance outcomes from coaching. Journal of Occupational and Organizational Psychology, 89(2), 249-277.

15. Gelb, M. (2000). How to Think Like Leonardo da Vinci: Seven Steps to Genius Every Day. Dell, New York, NY.

16. ChatOn. (2024, January 15). GPT-40 (Chat GPT AI) . https://chat.chaton.ai/

CHAPTER 2:

Think Strategically

Korn Ferry defines a strategic mindset as the ability to foresee future possibilities and translate them into breakthrough strategies. A strategic mindset is not just about thinking beyond the here and now; it's translating that thinking into breakthrough strategies that lead the organization into the future.[1]

New senior executives often struggle to take time to think and then act strategically, yet this is one of the most significant mindset changes required when you transition from senior manager to strategic leader. You have been comfortable and rewarded for doing: creating reports, delivering presentations, improving efficiency, and hitting quarterly milestones. While these capabilities are important for all leaders, strategic leaders must develop the habit of acting for the broader good and the longer term of the organization. The challenge for them is letting go of the doing themselves and facilitating the doing by coaching others.

A strategic mindset requires making decisions and setting direction that aligns with the overall objectives of the organization while accounting for internal dynamics, skills, culture, systems capabilities, and external environmental factors like supply chain, global unrest, market competition, and a myriad

She said, "think strategically "

of intangible variables. A strategic mindset requires moving from "here and now" to looking beyond the horizon and imagining what is possible.

> Acting strategically requires a holistic approach, considering broader contexts such as like market trends, competitor analysis, customer needs, and internal capabilities.

The concept of strategic thinking emerged in management literature in the early 20th century, with Peter Drucker's *Practice of Management* in 1954 and Michael Porter's Competitive Strategy in 1980. They argued that the purpose of strategic thinking is to discover novel, imaginative strategies which can rewrite the rules of the competitive game and envision futures that are significantly different from the present.[2]

Yet, a strategic mindset is hard to pin down or describe clearly. People often describe it to me as "I'll know it when I see it." But, this doesn't help the strategic leader develop this capability. I had a great conversation with Jason Mosakowski, a senior vice president at a global provider of employee engagement, customer loyalty, recognition, and reward services, about the challenges senior executives face in leaning into a strategic mindset. A strategic mindset is hard to pin down or describe clearly. It's often described as "I'll know it when I see it." "Some of us," he explained, "are more wired for a strategic, broader range view, while others are not naturally inclined to think in a strategic manner."[3]

Unclear what strategic orientation looks like? Strategic orientation can be measured with multiple assessments available on the market that identify differing propensities for strategic thinking. In the Meyer-Briggs Type Indicator[4], for example, Sensing individuals tend to focus on the details of a situation and are more oriented to the here and now, while Intuitives are more comfortable with abstract concepts and generally look toward the future. Clifton Strengths Finders assign their 31 "strengths" to one of four categories: Executing, Influencing, Relationship Building, and Strategic Thinking.[5] The Hogan Leadership Forecast Series utilizes the Inquisitive scale, among others, to ascertain one's propensity to think strategically.[6] While not definitive in identifying who is or isn't strategic, these tools provide valuable, highly validated scales and subscales that pinpoint how one is inclined or not inclined to be and act strategically.

Issues that strategic leaders face are often complex and novel. By cultivating a strategic mindset, executives can navigate complexity, drive innovation, and make more informed decisions. This requires the ability to prioritize and allocate resources effectively while also ensuring that the organization remains adaptable and resilient in the face of change.

Some key aspects of demonstrating a strategic mindset include:

Keeping abreast of external factors and translating that insight into tangible actions. I'm often surprised by how insulated senior executives can become. Yes, they attend their yearly sales and marketing summit, where they connect with other leaders inside the company, but many claim they are "too busy" to stay current in their industry. Are you networking regularly outside your firm? Are you attending national or international conferences to hear what's in development or what competitors are up to? Are you reading (or podcasting) academic research that provides perspective for your industry? A senior executive I work with regularly reminded me that this doesn't have to be done alone. Enlist your team in external outreach and then ensure they return and share a summary of what they discovered.

Developing and deploying a clear and compelling vision. What is your vision for the organization you lead, and specifically, how does your group impact the overall success of the organization? How are you going to influence your group to create breakthrough ideas that will address issues that are not here and now but over the horizon? Then, how will you communicate your progress against this vision to your team and other key stakeholders? Does your vision include enough specifics to avoid sweeping statements that might lead team members to question the veracity of the vision? Finally, does it specifically describe "why us?" How is our team specifically equipped, above all others, to provide its enabling capabilities for the organization?

Leveraging flexibility and adaptability. With global insights, strategic leaders recognize that the business landscape is constantly evolving. Are you willing to adapt to and adjust strategies as needed, no matter how well thought out they were? This involves setting targets, monitoring progress, evaluating outcomes, and making necessary and often significant adjustments to achieve long-range goals. Keep in mind that long-range goals generally don't change, but the strategies to achieve them often evolve over time.

Collaborating and communicating. Acting strategically also involves engaging and aligning stakeholders, both internal and external, to ensure a shared understanding of the strategic direction along with the rationale for that direction. Again, I'm surprised when I work on strategic projects with senior leaders who don't create a communication plan in the initial phases of a major project. Communication, they seem to think, happens when they are ready to implement. Highly capable strategic leaders draft key messages early in initiatives and revisit them throughout the project to make certain they hold true over time.

Executing and evaluating. Yes, great strategic leaders implement. They set milestones and track progress towards the desired outcomes. They leverage their team to identify methods for measuring progress, outcomes, and behavior changes, if needed. They champion regular evaluation and performance measurement to ensure their team identifies areas for improvement and makes informed decisions for future actions.

In summary, acting strategically involves critical thinking, long-term planning, and making decisions that align with the overall goals and objectives. It requires a combination of market intelligence, vision, adaptability, collaboration, and effective execution to drive success.

> A strategic mindset focuses on over-the-horizon solutions to address future challenges today.

WHAT MAKES STRATEGIC THINKING SO DIFFICULT?

Jason Mosakowski and I discussed the challenges leaders face in organizations when striving to act more strategically.

From his experience, he has discovered that so many senior leaders, even in the C-suite, are oriented on the here and now, the details and the repeatable processes that will deliver the immediate, expected results. He pointed out that we seem to have an inherent bias that focuses on the present rather than the longer term. He explained, "If I'm in an environment where longer-term orientation isn't valued, how do I get my colleagues on board for longer-term thinking when their bias is for tactical action?"

Below are some of the ways that hinder one's ability to stay within a strategic mindset. As you read, engage with these challenges. Which are most relevant, and how might they offer opportunities for your further growth and development?

Complexity of Decision-Making. Strategic thinking involves making decisions that have a significant impact on the organization's long-term success. Executives must navigate complex and multifaceted issues while considering various factors such as market trends, competitive landscape, financial implications, and organizational capabilities. The complexity of these decisions requires a deep understanding of the business, industry, and external environment. It must be made with a sense of urgency—not in the moment, but within a timeframe that will influence a successful outcome.

The challenge is that most of these issues are unclear now. Dozens of leaders have said to me, "I'm completely comfortable making this decision if I have confidence in how it's going to turn out." There's the rub, isn't it? Big, strategic, over-the-horizon decisions are filled with uncertainty and risk. It is easier and often safer to make short-term decisions where more is known; it takes courage to drive into the unknown.

Uncertainty and Ambiguity. A strategic mindset involves constantly dealing with uncertainty and ambiguity. Strategic leaders must analyze and interpret vast amounts of information, anticipate future trends, and make informed decisions despite incomplete or conflicting data. The uncertainty of the unknown weighs down many leaders, often preventing them from acting. Given more time, they believe, more information will be known and clarity revealed. This discomfort with ambiguity often keeps them in the here and now rather than a strategic framework.

Balancing Short-Term and Long-Term Priorities. Strategic leaders face the pressure of delivering short-term results while also focusing on long-term strategic goals. Balancing immediate operational demands with the need for long-term sustainability and growth is challenging. Focusing on long-term versus short-term goals requires a different set of mental activities, and many find it difficult to shift from one to the other at the moment. As one executive pointed out to me, long-term visions often require investment *now* that may lead to short-term financials actually being worse, making the investment case harder for others to swallow. Think of Amazon in its early years. Jeff Bezos didn't turn a profit at Amazon until its ninth year of operation; Ted Turner launched The Turner Communications Group in 1979. However, due to some aggressive and unsuccessful market acquisitions, Turner Broadcasting did not see an annual net profit until 1991, thanks in large part to CNN's coverage of Operation Desert Storm.[7]

Organizational Dynamics and Stakeholder Management. Executives must navigate organizational dynamics and manage various stakeholders with different interests and priorities. A strategic mindset involves aligning diverse perspectives, gaining buy-in from key stakeholders, and effectively communicating and implementing the strategic vision. This requires strong influencing skills, relationship-building, and time. It's easier to focus on the here-and-now decisions rather than invest in long-term stakeholder management that might not have an immediate return.

Overcoming Cognitive Biases. Like all individuals, strategic leaders are susceptible to cognitive biases that can cloud judgment and hinder effective strategic judgment. Biases such as confirmation bias, favoring information that confirms pre-existing beliefs; status quo bias, the ease of staying with what is comfortable and known; the availability heuristic, which is the tendency to utilize easily accessible information, impede objective analysis and decision-making. Overcoming these biases requires self-awareness, open-mindedness, and a willingness to challenge assumptions.

Solving World Hunger. I often use this expression tongue-in-cheek with executives I coach or senior teams I facilitate. As an effective strategic leader, it's easy to see how the parts connect with the whole and take on the large (and potentially unmanageable) challenges all at once. It's exciting to consider large, complex projects that will "move the needle" for the firm. Yet, they also have a high likelihood of failing or not delivering on expected results. Highly effective strategic leaders slice out the strategic work into projects with clear beginnings, middles, and ends so that the organization can reap benefits early, consistent benefits, and prevent resource overwhelm.

Jason Mosakowski recalls his time with a major multinational IT provider when he was asked to lead their India and South Asia regional operations. During his tenure in 2013 and 2014, the country was booming. Yet, the in-country team was underperforming in terms of revenue, profit, and market share. He, along with his American leaders, were expecting Jason to turn the business around. "Going in, I realized that we were underperforming based on the market potential, and I immediately wondered whether the team had the right strategy." He explained to me that he asked leaders for their business plans and was not surprised by what he found: "They were all short-term, annual operating plans. There was no strategy to guide them toward what market segments offered the best opportunities for profitable growth, what talent was required, what partnerships would be valuable to cultivate, and what sales and marketing strategies aligned with these growth objectives."

So, the team, along with Jason, set out to build a strategy. The challenge: getting people on board. The team was so operationally oriented that they had a hard time thinking about broader markets, the innovative solutions that his major multinational IT provider already provided that could be utilized in India, and what the economy was going to be like five years from now. As the team developed their plan, he was also challenged by getting the headquarters onboard. "We had to help them understand," he said, "that India was a different market. I had to educate them on local business practices to get them to understand that the plan would evolve differently than in other parts of the world. Yes, the quarterly execution was important, but we also identified the strategic milestones needed for our longer-term success." Jason's efforts were indeed successful. The results: in two years, the team was able to achieve 146% of the budget goals that were set in the plan, 30% year-to-year growth, and two points of market share gain.

As Jason shared his experience, I was reminded of my own experience living and working in China around the same time. I worked in Shanghai for Korn Ferry, and like many US and European-headquartered organizations, Korn Ferry viewed China as a "gold mine." They expected our revenue per consultant to be similar to, or even higher than, that in the U.S. They believed we could easily grow our local international presence because they felt there was an untapped need. It wasn't until the Korn Ferry president spent real time in China that he understood that the sales cycle was longer and that there was a sense amongst Chinese businesses of "just figuring it out" rather than utilizing the experience of an external consultancy. He realized that China's success was a long game rather than a matter of months.

BEHAVIORS LEADERS DEMONSTRATE WITH A STRATEGIC MINDSET

When strategic leaders engage in a strategic mindset, they demonstrate key behaviors. How regularly do you engage in the following?

Assess the frequency with which you demonstrate the following strategic mindset behaviors.	Rarely	Sometimes	Always
Ask questions that allow others to think about possibilities and options that have not yet been explored or tried.			
Take time to observe by not doing anything other than noticing your surroundings and what's going on.			
Articulate a credible picture of possibilities that will address unmet or underperforming needs.			
Engage in large, unwieldy projects where solutions and a path forward are less obvious.			
Facilitate the creation of competitive or breakthrough strategies that show a clear connection between vision and action.			
Find regular, uninterrupted time and space for your own deep thinking.			
Anticipate future trends and implications accurately by tapping into market intelligence outside the organization.			
Expose yourself to new ideas or perspectives through seminars, art exhibits, food experiences, or travel to out-of-the-ordinary global locations.			

A FRAMEWORK FOR A STRATEGIC MINDSET

We've discussed that acting strategically refers to the ability to think and plan for the long-term success of an organization. It involves making decisions and taking actions that align with overall goals and objectives while considering the external environment and influences. This, of course, is hard to do for the many dimensions I outlined above. As such, even strategic leaders settle back into the work and mindset that got them promoted to strategic leaders: doing. Doing includes the daily, tactical interactions that leaders engage in that are focused on the here and now, needing immediate attention.

While the list of behaviors above may be captivating, you may still be stuck in your day-to-day urgent priorities. One of my colleagues, a fellow coach, reviewed this chapter and shared that he was reminded of numerous leaders promoted to senior levels who were unable to make the mindset shift to strategic leaders. These highly engaged, energetic, and often well-liked individuals continued to get things done on their own, in their own comfort zone, not through others, but through their own exhaustive efforts. He calls them "super-managers."

One framework that I've found helpful with my executive coachees is the "being vs. doing" framework. First introduced by Peter Drucker in 1967 as "thinking vs. doing"[8], I was introduced to "being vs. doing" at my coaching certification program at Learning Journeys.[9] It evolved into a framework that helps leaders advancing through the executive ranks focus on more strategic, less tactical actions, *influencing* specific outcomes more than leading them directly.

Consider the following dimensions of being vs. doing.

Doing Focus	Being Focus
Behavioral Process: Doing refers to physical or behavioral actions that result from thoughts and intentions, including executing plans, making decisions, and engaging in activities.	**Cognitive Process:** Being involves mental processes and cognitive activities, such as problem-solving, considering options, influencing, imagining, analyzing, and reflecting.
Observable: Doing is typically observable by others and includes activities like talking, writing, producing, and monitoring.	**Internal Activity:** Being occurs within the mind and includes mental imagery, conceptualization, memory use, and application of knowledge.
Outcome-Oriented: Doing is about achieving tangible results or outcomes. It involves taking steps to turn thoughts and intentions into reality.	**Preparation:** It is often a precursor to action. It involves generating ideas, considering options, and evaluating potential courses of action.
Requires Energy: Doing often requires physical energy and effort, involving active engagement with the external world, listening and responding.	**Can Appear to be Passive:** While leaders in a "being attitude" may not actively contribute to the conversation, they take in and reflect on what's being said, applying those insights later.
Timely: Doing is time-bound and often has a sense of immediacy. It's about acting in the present moment or according to a schedule.	**Influences Action:** Being is not an idle activity; the time spent can lead to new conceptualizations that can be translated into actions.

I introduced the concept of being vs. doing to Bob Ehren, a senior vice president at a major financial services organization, early in our coaching relationship[10]. An actuarial by training, Bob, years ago when we all dressed more formally at work, kept a spreadsheet for his professional wardrobe—ties, shirts, suits, jackets—so in the morning, he didn't have to consider what to wear or, more importantly, when he last wore his blue herringbone shirt or charcoal grey suit. In our years working together, I discovered he is a truly trusted advisor within the firm. The CEO repeatedly told me that Bob was one of his key go-to people, someone who fully and deeply understood the interconnected financial implications, risks, and their likelihood of occurring.

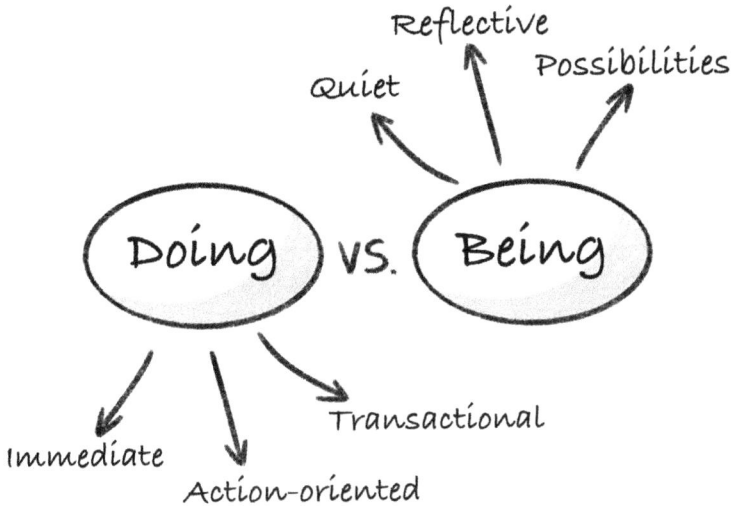

Reflective
Quiet
Possibilities

Doing vs. Being

Immediate
Action-oriented
Transactional

When Bob and I first started working together, he was a highly regarded senior executive because of his knowledge and experience, but he often found himself constantly being pulled into operational issues—solving staff conflicts, creating analyses for the executive team, and helping the organization navigate through COVID. We would sometimes say he was "stuck in first gear." The being vs. doing framework permitted him to spend time considering longer-term implications and initiatives. He realized that *being* time didn't have to result in a spreadsheet or a PowerPoint presentation but could simply be the formulation of a concept or idea to share with his colleagues later. Reflecting on the framework, Bob shared, "Being vs doing positively changed how I viewed leadership. The clarity of where (and when) I should be 'being' to drive outcomes through counsel, advice, and direction (versus other actions) not only helped me be more impactful as a leader but also empowered others around me."

A STRATEGIC MINDSET CHAMPION

I was introduced to Skip Dye, where I often get introduced to new and refreshing concepts and leaders while listening to a podcast during a workout. Skip is the Senior Vice President of Library Sales and Digital Strategy at Penguin Random House, one of the world's largest booksellers.[11] Skip's job is to sell and market books to teachers and librarians. Last year, Skip provided an update to his board of directors on the impact book banning was having on the company. According to Skip's account, it became an impassioned discussion because book banning was not only impacting Penguin Random House's bottom line, but also authors and students as the trend grew. From July 2021 to July 2022, for example, over 1,500 books were banned across U.S. schools and libraries, with Penguin Random House having more titles on banned lists than any other publisher.[12] While sales were impacted, Skip noted that authors were also being impacted—discouraged from writing about sensitive content or being disinvited from making appearances at schools and libraries.

Historically, Penguin Random House had financially supported advocacy groups fighting book bans, but these efforts hadn't made a measurable impact. At the board meeting, Skip was charged with acting. He was not given specific actions but instead given guidance by the CEO to "do something significant," a strategic task. Skip formed the Intellectual Freedom Task Force within Penguin Random House. Their work began by joining an existing lawsuit underway brought about by teachers and students in Florida's Escambia School District. They then sued the state of Iowa for limiting access to books as a violation of the free speech and equal protection clauses of the U.S. Constitution; Penguin Random House believed authors had the right to communicate to students without undue interference from the government.

While suing state governments over book banning was a risky decision, Skip agreed it was the right thing to do. It wasn't just a financial issue, he said, but a free speech and access issue. When Skip set out on the auspicious goal of requiring states to stop banning books, there was no clear outcome. Skip believed Penguin Random House was "offering stewardship to good authors with voices people want to hear." He reminded the interviewer that Random House is not imposing an ideology or viewpoint on what readers should or shouldn't read but rather ensuring the freedom to read and have access to all who choose to read.

Had Skip adopted a "doing" mindset rather than thinking, the impact of book banning most likely would have been far less significant. Penguin Random House is not a litigious organization. Taking on some of the school districts, which were some of the largest customers, had numerous pitfalls. Skip could have taken the board's direction and done much of the same, but only more, fitting in with strategies that had previously been deployed and accepted by senior leadership.

However, Skip's approach was strategic. His success was not clear at the beginning of the initiative, and he invested dollars that were most likely not budgeted and could result in protracted and unclear outcomes. Yet, like so many who possess or develop a strategic mindset, Skip didn't set out to take on some of the largest school districts in the country; he set out to solve an issue of access to literature.

PRACTICES FOR DEVELOPING A STRATEGIC MINDSET HABIT

Developing a strategic mindset isn't a skills-based exercise, which is why I refer to it as a mindset. Yet, those of us in the talent development field believe that a mindset for strategy can be developed. It doesn't occur by following steps 1, then 2, then 3. Rather, it happens through exposing yourself to less ordinary or less comfortable but challenging experiences and environments. Consider the following as you work to expand your strategic mindset.

Read, read, read. Or listen, listen, listen. Strategic thinking books abound; a quick Amazon search yielded over 60 books! Podcasts and TEDTalks also yield a plethora of insights on expanding your thinking, challenging your own status quo, and considering alternative constructs. Be patient on your journey. As one executive reminded me years ago, "Janet, I don't generally have a breakthrough by reading a single book or article. It's the addictive nature from multiple viewpoints that form altering perspectives for me."

Engage with diverse perspectives. Be intentional about it, as I have found this doesn't come naturally to many people. Engage in discussions and actively seek diverse perspectives from colleagues, mentors, and industry experts. Attend conferences that aren't at the center of your industry. Find a new interest group or forum (online or live) that advocates for positions other than your own. Join a non-profit board of directors in your local community to share your highly developed skills. Listen, more than share, when you're in these surroundings. Take notes for later reflection. Share what you discover with someone else.

Analyze case studies. Analyzing real-world case studies can help you understand how successful strategies are formulated and implemented. Longtime professor and business executive Nitin Nohria discussed the value of reviewing case studies. He recalled that Harvard Business School has been using the case study method for nearly 100 years. Beyond teaching specific subject matter, he asserted, the case study method excels in instilling meta-skills, such as judgment, bias recognition, and curiosity.[13] Harvard Business School offers a wide range of case studies that can be a valuable resource for enhancing your strategic thinking skills. Case studies are powerful on their own but are even more useful when explored by a group of colleagues. Most importantly, however, do something with your insights. What are your takeaways from the case? How do they apply to your current situation? Capture your insights on a post-it note and keep it nearby as a reminder to make it real.

Utilize breakthrough thinking techniques. "But I'm not creative," I've heard from many executives. My response is, "You don't have to be." Individuals with a strategic mindset surround themselves with breakthrough thinkers or facilitate breakthrough conversations themselves. Abandon simple brainstorming; instead, utilize online or live techniques that challenge people to think differently about situations. See the chapter on gaining comfort with ambiguity for specific tools and techniques.

Practice systems thinking. It involves understanding the interconnectedness of various components and how they impact the overall system. Ask questions about upstream and downstream impacts and describe the inputs and outputs of a process to understand the whole picture, not just its parts. Use systems thinking language with your team to help them understand its value.

Seek international assignments. I have found that a distinct difference exists between leaders who have worked internationally and those who haven't. Whether living abroad with your family or alone, working in another country—particularly one that doesn't primarily speak English—requires you to solve both work and living challenges, adapt to different economies, and experience life and work in unexpected ways. International work assignments allow you to acquire unique and highly valued perspectives, such as adaptability, problem-solving in diverse environments, multicultural collaboration, and the ability to perform under pressure.[14]

A FEW COMMENTS ABOUT INTERNATIONAL WORK EXPERIENCES

Perhaps I'm biased about the value of international work

experiences because my own experience of living and working in China was so informative and mind-opening. Simply put, international work experience allows you to see things differently and challenge your paradigms.

Lisa Dragoni et al.[15] examined the relationship between a leader's global work experience and their strategic thinking capabilities. Dragoni and her colleagues evaluated the strategic competency of 231 upper-level leaders in terms of a leader's financial acumen, innovative thinking, analytic business judgment, and global perspective. These leaders possessed international work experience, either by heading up functional departments or serving as business unit leaders in non-home country settings. Their analysis revealed that the time leaders spent in global work experiences was positively correlated with their strategic thinking competency. Further, developing strategic thinking skills becomes even more significant when leaders have their international experiences in culturally distant countries.

The Korn Ferry Assessment of Leadership Potential assesses an individual's leadership potential by measuring leadership capability irrespective of the leader's current position. It uses multiple signposts of leadership potential—motivation drivers, self-awareness, learning agility, and logical reasoning—to identify a leader's potential to develop the qualities required for effective performance in a significantly more challenging leadership role. It looks at a leader's capacity for long-term growth, focusing on the person's aptitudes, personality traits, mindset, motivation, and values. Within the assessment, the leader is asked to describe formative work experiences and long-term international assignments. The researchers at Korn Ferry have validated that the broader work experience you have, including the dramatic impact international assignments have on your career, the more likely you are to be successful in highly challenging, strategic situations.[16]

Yes, international assignments are great — indeed, life-changing — but they can also be hard to come by. When supported by multinational organizations, Harvard researchers estimated that it could cost two to three times an employee's salary for a fully funded expatriate assignment. Most of us can't afford to simply quit our jobs, move to a foreign country, and hope to find gainful employment. Yet, there are options.

- **Consider an extended volunteer effort.** Many local churches offer three and four-day mission trips to communities in Mexico—so why not consider extending your stay? Take a month from your job and live and work in that community, explore the language, and live off the economy. Some employers even provide paid leave for this kind of "greater good" initiative.

- **Seek short-term rotational assignments.** While working in China, I discovered that a client, Johnson and Johnson, had a unique approach to international assessments. They offered employees in Asia a three-month assignment in another Asian country. Often, two employees would switch roles, doubling the assignment's impact. It seemed like a win for everyone. The company didn't bear the cost of moving the employee's family elsewhere, although JNJ did allow the leader one home visit and the employee's family one visit to the country where the leader was working during the three months. Employees lived in the economy and discovered how things were done elsewhere. They, in turn, brought these insights and perspectives back to their home office at the end of the assignment.

- **Seek out international projects.** Many organizations have a global reach. They have teams in myriad countries doing dimensions or sub-components of the organization's work. Seek these out and volunteer to be part of an international team. If given the opportunity to travel to where the team is, suspend the tendency to make the trip a "quick turn" because of your priorities at home. Extend your visit and experience the local economy without a tour guide. Spend a few weeks on-site working with the team to develop relationships and understand their work from their perspective.

After living and working in Shanghai, China, for three years, I discovered the incredible, life-altering perspectives it created. There are countless ways to expand your international under-standing. While these experiences may not fully replace the benefits of physically living abroad, they can provide valuable insights, knowledge, and cross-cultural skills that are highly valued in today's globalized world. Can't take advantage of some of these options, get out of your comfort zone locally. Take a world religions or governments class at a local college. Seek out visiting professor's talks. Look for volunteer work in your local community that has an international connection.

PUTTING IT INTO ACTION

Review the simple assessment you completed above.

What **one** habit or practice would you like to be practicing to advance your strategic mindset?	What are you willing to **give up** on adopting this practice?

REFERENCES

1. https://www.kornferry.com.
2. Drucker, P. (1954). Practice of Management. Harper Business; Porter, M. (1980). Competitive Strategy: Techniques for Analyzing Industries and Competitors. Free Press.
3. Mosakowski, J. (February 23, 2024). Conversation with Janet Polach. linkedin.com/in/jason-mosakowski.
4. https://en.wikipedia.org/wiki/Myers%E2%80%93Briggs_Type_Indicator.
5. https://www.gallup.com/cliftonstrengths/en/252137/home.aspx.
6. https://www.hoganassessments.com/products/leadership-forecast-series/
7. Hendrick, D., (2014, July 7,). 5 successful companies that didn't make a dollar for 5 years. Inc., https://www.inc.com/drew-hendricks/5-successful-companies-that-didn-8217-t-make-a-dollar-for-5-years.html.
8. Drucker, P. F. (1967). *The Effective Executive: The Definitive Guide to Getting the Right Things Done*. HarperCollins Publishers.
9. https://www.learningjourneys.net/
10. Erhren, B. (2023). Ongoing conversations with Janet Polach. linkedin.com/in/bob-ehren.
11. Trachtenberg, J. A. (February 27, 2024). Inside one publisher's fight against book bans. The Journal. https://www.wsj.com/podcasts/the-journal/inside-one-publishers-fight-against-book-bans/26540004-b6b8-43eb-8401-76669af321db
12. Trachtenberg, J. A. (January 27, 2024). A publishing giant's risky fight against book bans. The Wall Street Journal. https://www.wsj.com/arts-culture/books/penguin-random-house-book-ban-publishing-giant-risky-fight-230eb685?reflink=share_mobilewebshare
13. Shiller International University. (July 25, 2023). The value of international work experience in a globalized world. https://schiller.edu/the-value-of-international-work-experience-in-a-globalized-world#:~:text=Gaining%20Unique%20Professional%20Skills%3A%20International,ability%20to%20work%20under%20pressure.

14 Nohria, N. (2021, December 21). What the case study method really teaches. Harvard Business Review. https://hbr.org/2021/12/what-the-case-study-method-really-teaches

15 Dragoni, L., I.-S., Tesluk, P.E., Moore, O.A., VanKatwyk, P., & Hazucha, J. (2014). Developing a leader's strategic thinking through global work experience: The moderating role of cultural distance. Journal of Applied Psychology, 99(5). 867–882.

16 www.kornferry.com. https://www.kornferry.com/insights/featured-topics/leadership/essential-guide-to-leadership-assessments

CHAPTER 3:

Empower Managers

Fundamentally, strategic leaders must allow their managers to manage. To do this, they must set expectations, meet with their managers regularly, and encourage them to put their ideas to improve the effectiveness of processes and teams. Leaders must adopt a mindset that their way is not the only way to get things done. By allowing their managers to manage truly, they develop their manager's skills, enhance their own capacity as strategic leaders, and prepare managers for the next level of leadership.

Yet, allowing managers to manage runs into numerous challenges for the senior leader. Leaders may struggle to trust their managers to take on more responsibilities and independent decision-making, feeling the need to maintain control or finding it difficult to delegate authority. The existing organizational culture can also pose challenges to empowering managers. In a hierarchical or change-resistant culture, leaders may face opposition when trying to empower managers and distribute decision-making authority downward. Furthermore, leaders often find themselves busy with their own responsibilities. They may struggle to find the time to empower and support their managers effectively.

One senior executive reminded me that to delegate and

empower others, she needed to maintain appropriate levels of communication with her managers. While she wasn't doing their initiative or project, her boss, she pointed out, would still likely ask her about the progress. Being confident that things are under control would allow her to share that confidence with her peers and her executives.[1]

There's a balance between gathering enough information to support your direct report and avoiding micromanaging. Overcoming these challenges requires a mindset shift in leaders to understand the importance of empowerment, communicate effectively, build trust, and align the organization's culture with the goals of their empowered managers.

Put another way, strategic leaders empowering their managers is like giving a newly appointed driver the keys to a car. Just as a car provides the freedom to travel and explore new destinations, empowering managers gives them the authority and resources to make decisions and lead their teams. It allows managers to navigate challenges, drive innovation, and take ownership of their responsibilities, ultimately propelling the organization forward.

However, it's not always easy. That same senior executive pointed out that sometimes the organization doesn't trust the input from lower-level managers, expecting the senior leader to solve the problem and make the decision. If, for example, the director or their direct reports do not possess the skills or confidence to speak up and lead, a highly capable strategic leader might fill the void in the conversation, which then results in people directing the conversation back to them. Too often, senior executives empower someone, but at the first sign of struggle, they pull the power back. This is absolutely deflating for the manager and obviously leads to sub-optimal results.

As a strategic leader, you need to ensure that your managers have the necessary skills, knowledge, and resources to make decisions effectively. Yet, the leader must let go and trust that the manager will be responsible, just like trusting a driver with a car.

Ultimately, strategic leaders face the challenge of empowering their managers to make decisions while ensuring the stability and success of both the initiative and the organization. You may ask, "Aren't these the same considerations for empowering frontline employees?" Yes, but with empowering managers, the stakes and visibility are much higher.

Behaviors of an Empowering Strategic Leader: When strategic leaders empower managers well, they demonstrate key behaviors. How well do you do this?

Assess the frequency you demonstrate the following "empowering managers" behaviors.	Rarely	Sometimes	Always
Trust your managers to make decisions and take ownership of their decisions.			
Create a regular two-way communication process to facilitate check-ins on progress and address barriers.			
Spend more time listening than talking to learn how the manager/director plans to accomplish the assigned task or make a decision.			
Delegate meaningful responsibilities to your managers/directors, and don't step in when the manager reaches a roadblock or obstacle.			
Be available for questions and collaborate with the manager/director.			

Assess the frequency you demonstrate the following "empowering managers" behaviors.	Rarely	Sometimes	Always
Give the manager/director time to learn and make mistakes.			
Hold the manager/director accountable for both timelines and outcomes related to the assigned task, project, or decision.			
Ask the manager/director what they are learning and what they might do differently next time.			
Communicate desired outcomes and metrics to guide your managers' work.			

> To be a highly effective strategic leader, you don't have to do ALL of the behaviors all of the time. Instead, pick a few to focus on and develop a mindset for empowering managers.

WHAT GETS IN THE WAY OF EMPOWERING OTHERS

Barriers to empowering our less experienced leaders exist; some are imposed by the organization, and others by ourselves.

Lack of Trust. One of the key barriers to empowering managers is a lack of trust between strategic leaders and their junior leaders. When you don't trust your managers to make important decisions or take on additional responsibilities, you are less likely to empower them. This lack of trust can stem from various factors, like a fear of losing control or a belief that managers may not have the necessary skills or expertise. According to Spreitzer and Mishra,[2] trust is crucial for empowering managers as it allows leaders to delegate authority and responsibilities effectively.

We often think of trust as binary: we either trust someone or we don't. Extending trust is a clear decision for strategic leaders. But they often can't determine why they do or don't trust someone. Trust is based on experience and interactions. Charles Feltman's, The Thin Book of Trust[3] outlines four key elements of trust.

- **Care.** You have the other person's interest in mind when you make decisions or take action.

- **Sincerity.** You are honest and act with genuineness; you say what you mean and mean what you say.

- **Reliability.** You meet the commitments that you made; you keep your promises.

- **Competence.** You are competent in your duties.

As a strategic leader, you must assess whether you trust one of your managers with a key initiative. The framework above is useful for defining why you do or don't trust others. This assessment then allows you to determine the steps needed to ensure the manager's success with a delegated responsibility. After completing this assessment of a manager, I encourage you to have a conversation with them, sharing your results and discussing ways to improve the trust relationship together.

Micromanagement. Some leaders may be hesitant to delegate authority and decision-making responsibilities out of fear of losing control over the outcome or the path to the decision. They may not feel uncomfortable giving up power. They may worry that managers will make decisions that go against "the way I would do it." This fear can hinder the empowerment process, limiting the growth and development of others.

What does micromanagement look like?

- ♟ Assigning a task to a manager and then frequently checking in to assess progress and offer suggestions.

- ♟ Correcting the way the manager is proceeding on a task or project.

- ♟ Using expressions like, "I've done this before, and for me, this is what works best." Or, "Can I suggest you try this or that instead of your approach?"

- ♟ Asking for daily updates on progress.

While some of these behaviors are suitable for a manager delegating to a frontline employee, they may not be appropriate for a strategic leader.

Micromanagement occurs when strategic leaders excessively control and monitor their managers' work, leaving little room for autonomy or decision-making. This can hinder the empowerment of managers by limiting their ability to take ownership of their work and make independent decisions. Further, it also doesn't allow the strategic leader to work on higher-level strategies if they are spending all their time micromanaging. Research by Deci and Ryan[4] suggested that micromanagement can undermine intrinsic motivation and job satisfaction, ultimately hindering managers' confidence.

A longtime friend and senior executive said it so well, "As a senior leader, I placed more value on being an expert and getting the work done than I did on building up the team. Part of this was permitting failure. As a strategic leader, you challenge your thinking when you have the inclination to get involved. Getting things "right" is the manager's job. Building capability and growing diverse approaches is the strategic leader's job.

Lack of Clear Communication. Effective empowerment requires clear communication between strategic leaders and managers. If there is a lack of clarity regarding expectations, goals, decision-making authority, and timeline, managers may struggle to make informed decisions.

Empowering others in decision-making is not a "set it and forget it" effort. Clear communication channels must be established and maintained throughout the process to ensure that managers have the information and resources they need to make empowered decisions. Are you establishing a weekly or bi-weekly cadence? Are you using tools like MS Notes to share ongoing insights or track progress? How are you making this check-in process more deliberate and visible to both you and your direct report leaders?

Effective communication and feedback are essential for empowering managers. When strategic leaders fail to provide clear expectations, guidance, and feedback, it can lead to confusion, frustration, and a lack of confidence in decision-making. Sharing "philosophies" to guide the work and

discussing key issues that inhibit execution is another strategy. Keep in mind that communication is two-way. Communication between a manager and strategic leader allows strategic leaders to know what the manager is doing; is the project going to plan, without having to attend meetings to hear others assess whether the project is on track? According to Conger and Kanungo,[5] regular and open communication between leaders and managers is critical for empowerment. It helps managers understand strategic goals, align their actions, and make informed decisions. Being "too busy" is not an excuse for skipping regular one-on-one meetings with each of your managers.

Reluctance to Change. Empowering managers may involve a shift in organizational culture and traditional hierarchies. Some leaders may resist this change, especially if they are used to top-down decision-making approaches. Managers may feel unclear about the request, uncomfortable with the novelty of the experience, lack confidence in their own judgement, or simply not want the extra work.

Lack of Skills. Empowered managers need adequate training and support to effectively handle their increased authority and decision-making responsibilities. Without proper training or experience, managers may feel overwhelmed or unsure of how to make informed decisions. Learning programs that include decision-making models, option evaluation, and identifying decision criteria are a must to help managers gain confidence in their own skills. Check yourself, though. Are you using "lack of skills" as an excuse, or are you simply reluctant to give up control?

Fear of Mistakes and Failures. Empowering managers means giving them the freedom to make decisions, which inherently carries the risk of mistakes and failures. Some leaders may be hesitant to empower managers out of fear of negative consequences. However, it's important to recognize that mistakes and failures are part of the learning process. Foster an organization that views mistakes as opportunities for growth and encourages managers to learn from their experiences. After all, most decisions won't bring the organization crashing down.

> For the new or unproven manager, empowerment may require more time from the strategic leader.

Addressing these challenges requires a proactive approach from strategic leaders and a commitment to creating a supportive, empowering environment. By recognizing and overcoming these challenges, organizations can successfully empower managers and benefit from their increased autonomy and decision-making capabilities. This is, in fact, a strategic leader's most valuable output.

BENEFITS OF EMPOWERING MANAGERS

Empowering managers does not yield immediate results; it requires a mindset shift. It begins by assigning low-impact tasks to develop skills and build trust in others. Then it becomes more sweeping, as broader organization accepts empowering others. When you empower others well, it allows you to spend more time on strategic work and cross-organizational collaboration. So, with effort on the part of the strategic leader, both the leader and the organization benefit.

Increased innovation. Empowering managers encourages creative thinking and risk-taking. When managers have the freedom to explore new ideas and experiment with different approaches, they are more likely to come up with innovative solutions and strategies. This fosters a culture of innovation across the organization, leading to potential competitive advantages in the market. For additional perspectives on innovation, refer to the chapter on embracing ambiguity.

Manager development. Strategic leaders who empower their managers prioritize development. By delegating responsibilities and providing opportunities for growth, managers can develop their skills, capabilities, and confidence. This not only benefits the individual managers but also creates a pipeline of talent within the organization, ensuring a strong leadership bench for the future.

Better resource utilization. Empowered managers have a deeper understanding of their team's capabilities and resource needs. They can make informed decisions about resource allocation, ensuring that resources are effectively utilized to achieve strategic objectives. This helps the organization optimize its resources and achieve better results.

Enhanced decision-making. Empowered managers are closer to the issues and the people responsible for implementing solutions. This enables managers to make timely decisions based on their own expertise and knowledge. As a result, you can rely on your manager to make informed decisions that align with the organization's goals and strategies.

Enhance manager well-being. Empowering leadership positively influences employees' psychological well-being by enhancing their sense of competence, autonomy, and relatedness, as reported by Tuckey et al.[6] Managers who are truly allowed to make decisions, have them stick, and follow a process that they deem appropriate, feel more in control and engaged with the organization as a whole. They feel more committed to their leader, as the leader allows them to complete work as they see fit, thus improving retention rates. By empowering managers, strategic leaders create a culture of trust, collaboration, and accountability, ultimately driving the organization's success.

THE DARK SIDE OF EMPOWERING LEADERS

Of course, there are always downsides to empowerment, and they are well-documented in the research. Lin et al.,[7] Dennerlein and Krikman,[8] and Cheong et al.[9] have all explored the darker side of empowerment. Yes, there is deep and plentiful research on the value of empowering managers, yet there are a few potential drawbacks. First, empowered managers may engage in shady or unethical behaviors in trying to achieve the empowered goals. Managers given lofty goals or have been assigned high expectations may "push the limits" of acceptable practices within the organization or skirt the rules to achieve within the assigned goals or timelines. While these individuals may not be wholly unethical, they might cut corners, inflate prices, or adjust performance outputs to achieve aspirational goals.

Dennerlein and Kirkman[8] discovered that there are two dimensions to empowerment: *enabling processes*—leaders who literally enable their team toward self-efficacy and performance because they have established reasonable and achievable goals—and *burdening processes*, which diminish the positive influence of empowerment, resulting in job-induced tension and higher levels of stress. While these negative outcomes are never desired, their likelihood can be significantly reduced by strategic leaders who establish guidelines for the empowered tasks or projects and engage in regular progress checks on successes and challenges, working closely with the empowered to address challenges.

POTENTIAL PRACTICES FOR DEVELOPING A MINDSET FOR EMPOWERING MANAGERS

Review the mindset shifts below. In any developmental process, not all changes can be adopted simultaneously. Select one or two that would help you develop a mindset for empowering your managers.

Potential Practices	Interested in Development 5 = highly interested 1 = minimally interested
Create self-talk that reminds you that you don't have all the answers and that others can do projects, but not necessarily your own way.	
Accept that the time you spend in empowerment develops others' skills and confidence and ultimately leads to success.	
Become aware of your talk-to-listening ratio. Challenge yourself to speak no more than 30% of the meeting. Allow the initiative or delegated manager to set up and lead the meeting, allowing you to act as an SME or influencer.	
Check-in on the stress level of the empowered, ensuring they are not "pushing the rules" just to succeed. Openly discuss feelings and worries with the delegated manager.	

Potential Practices	Interested in Development 5 = highly interested 1 = minimally interested
Let go of micromanaging. You don't have to know all the details; focus on the general direction, timelines, and reiterate the goals.	
Tap into optimistic, encouraging people. Discuss what's possible rather than what's not.	
Work with managers on creating success for a newly delegated task. Establish goals, timelines, and identify regular check-in dates up front.	
Introduce your managers to senior leaders before they need to present or own an issue. Invite them to broader organizational meetings when opportunities arise and establish them as experts before assigning them an empowered project.	
"Gameplay" high-risk decisions to allow leaders to understand possibilities and risks, but don't make decisions for them.	
Engage with the empowered manager to ascertain whether the empowerment process is working for them, and ask for changes or enhancements.	

PUTTING IT INTO ACTION

What **one** habit or practice would you like to adopt to advance your empowering manager mindset?	What are you willing to **give up** to adopt this practice?

REFERENCES

1. Tucker, K. (2024, May 22). linkedin.com/in/kristine-tucker-9b75483.

2. Spreitzer, G. M., & Mishra, A. K. (2002). To empower or not to empower your sales force? An empirical examination of the influence of leadership empowerment behavior on customer satisfaction and performance. *Journal of Applied Psychology*, 87(5), 971-979.

3. Feltman, C., (2021). *The thin book of trust: An essential primer for building trust at work*, 2nd ed. The Thin Book Publishing. Bend, OR.

4. Deci, E. L., & Ryan, R. M. (2000). The "what" and "why" of goal pursuits: Human needs and the self-determination of behavior. *Psychological Inquiry*, 11(4), 227-268.

5. Conger, J. A., & Kanungo, R. N. (1998). Charismatic leadership in organizations: Perceived behavioral attributes and their measurement. *Journal of Organizational Behavior*, 19(2), 147-167.

6. Tuckey, M.R., Bakker, A. B., Dollard, M. F., Hurrell, J. J. (2012). Empowering leaders optimize working conditions for engagement: A multilevel study. Journal of Occupational Health and Psychology, 17(1), 15-17.

7. Lin, S., Chen, S., & Liu, X., (2023). The dark side of empowering leadership: How empowering leadership affects unethical pro-organization behavior in construction projects. Buildings, 13(10), p. 2640.

8. Dennerlein, T., & Kirkman, B. L., (2002). The hidden dark side of empowering leadership: The moderating role of hindrance stressors in explaining when empowering employees can promote moral disengagement and unethical pro-organizational behavior. Journal of Applied Psychology, 107(12), 2220–2242. https://doi-org.ezp1.lib.umn.edu/10.1037/apl0001013.

9. Cheong, M. Spain, S. M., Yammarino, F. J., & Seokhwa, Y. (2016), The two faces of empowering leadership: Enabling and burdening. *The Leadership Quarterly*, 27(4), 602-616.

CHAPTER 4

Listen More Thank Talk

In the dynamic and ever-evolving business world, strategic leaders are constantly challenged to effectively communicate and connect with their teams, clients, and stakeholders. One crucial aspect often overlooked is the power of listening. Researchers have discovered that executives who prioritize and excel in listening are more likely to foster trust, build stronger relationships, and make better-informed decisions. A study conducted by Itzchak and Kluger[1] at Harvard found that leaders who are effective listeners are perceived as being more competent and trustworthy by their employees. This chapter explores the challenges and strategies for effectual listening. We will clarify the mindset shift required to be a highly effective strategic listener, delve into the significance of listening as a leadership skill, explore the science behind active listening, and provide practical strategies to enhance your listening abilities. Prepare to unlock the transformative potential of listening and elevate your listening effectiveness as an executive leader.

How well you listen significantly impacts your effectiveness as a strategic leader and the quality of the relationships you develop. We listen for many reasons: to obtain information, to understand or confirm information, to learn something new, and for pure enjoyment. What is effective listening? Scholars and the popular press have described the ability and willingness to listen as active listening fully. Specifically, active listening is making a conscious effort to hear not only the words another person is saying but also the complete message that the speaker is communicating.

Yet, in today's chaotic world, listening is a challenge. We've come to expect soundbites from the media, social or other-wise, rather than patiently listening to the whole story. We IM others with headlines rather than taking a moment to walk to their workspace to engage in a real conversation. It's become common place to have side conversations during meetings. Said one senior leader, "If it is a real meeting, why would we be whispering in each other's ear? Why is the chat ok?" Further, we play our podcasts at an accelerated speed or while writing emails or doing housework to double our productivity. We've become desensitized to sincere listening: making real mean-ing from sound.

Yet, listening is fundamental to the work strategic leaders do. Consider the following.

- Lee and Hatesohl estimated that in America, we spend 70 to 80 percent of our time in some form of communication. Of that time, we spend about 9 percent writing, 16 percent reading, 30 percent speaking, and 45 percent listening.[2]

- Over time, studies have confirmed that most of us are poor and inefficient listeners.[3]

- More than 50% of managers do not listen to their employees in an effective manner.[3]

- On average, workers spend 55 percent of their workday listening, and managers spend about 63 percent listening.[4]

- Yet less than 2% of the workforce has had formal listening training.[5]

♟ We remember only 25 to 30% of what we hear.[6]

♟ Employees who feel listened to are 4.6 times more likely to feel empowered to perform their best work.[6]

> **Hearing is the physical process that allows us to perceive sound through our ears; active listening happens mentally when we concentrate on a sound to derive meaning from it.**

Fully listening to someone builds relationships. Listening, however, is more than connecting with others and showing you care. High-quality listening helps speakers see both sides of an argument. Itzchakov and Kluger considered the impact of poor and effective listening on college students. 1 When they paired speakers with "good" listeners, as defined by being solely focused on the speaker, encouraging non-verbal communication, and paraphrasing what was heard, speakers felt less anxious, more self-aware, and reported higher clarity about their attitudes on the topics. Speakers paired with undistracted listeners reported wanting to share their point of view with other people more compared with speakers paired with distracted listeners. They discovered from additional research that when they paired workers with high, medium, or low-quality listeners, managers who listened to their employees talk about their own experiences before receiving feedback can make the worker feel higher psychological safety and become less defensive.

Effective Leaders:

70% / 30%

listen   speak

Daniel Goleman popularized the concept of emotional intelligence in 1995[7]. First conceived by researchers Peter Salovey and John Mayer in 1990[8], who described EQ as a social intelligence that involves monitoring one's and others' feelings and emotions, discriminating amongst them, and using that information to guide one's thinking and interactions. Emotional Intelligence has been attributed to interpersonal and leadership success because it requires the individual to successfully interact with others, not just on a cognitive level, but on an emotional level. Goldman, Salovey, and Mayer have successfully argued that connecting with others on an emotional level allows the strategic leader to interact on a deeper level, thereby building trust and assurance when two individuals interact.

At the heart of emotional intelligence is active, empathetic listening. Active, empathetic listening is the active and emotional involvement of the listener during a given interaction. It is an involvement that is conscious on the listener's part but is also perceived by the speaker.[7]

Goleman[9], who continues to research the power of interactive listening, penned a short post on LinkedIn where he reaffirmed the three stages of effective listening: sensing, processing, and responding:

- **Sensing.** Understanding how the other person feels or reacts and picking up on unspoken cues, such as body language, is often described as empathy.

- **Processing.** Remembering what the other person said, asking for clarification as needed, and reflecting on the other person's perspective in your own thinking.

- **Responding.** Being actively involved while the other person is speaking, such as making eye contact, nodding, or smiling, as well as paraphrasing and asking questions that show you are engaged.

Actively listening empathetically is not easy to do and can even be stressful. In my leadership development programs, I facilitate an exercise that is quite insightful. Two partners select a mildly controversial issue: a local road construction project, climate change solutions, one sports team over another, the best country to travel to, and the best ways to stay healthy. I encourage participants to stay away from highly controversial and emotional topics such as abortion, gun control, or international politics. In the pair, Person A describes their own position clearly and succinctly. Person B then paraphrases their partner's position on the issue. In the debrief, participants are amazed at how difficult this seemingly simple exercise can be. They report inevitably falling into the trap of focusing on what they might say next or how best to counter the other person's perspective rather than simply listening and summarizing. They also describe experiencing a great deal of stress while listening to their partner to make sure they "get it right." When strategic leaders adopt a listening more than talking mindset, they become open to other's ideas and perspectives that they may not have previously considered.

Put another way, listening is like a key that unlocks the door to relationship development. Just as a key allows you to enter a room and explore its contents, effective listening allows you to enter someone's world and understand their thoughts, feelings, and experiences. When you genuinely listen to another person, you show them you value and respect their perspective. It creates a safe and open space for them to share their thoughts and emotions while fostering trust and connection. Just as exploring an unfamiliar room reveals hidden treasures, listening reveals insights, emotions, and deeper layers of understanding in a relationship. By actively listening, you can build a stronger foundation for communication, empathy, mutual understanding, and decision-making, ultimately fostering the relationship's growth.

LISTENING IMPACTS EFFECTIVE DECISION-MAKING

Active listening involves giving full attention to the speaker and seeking to understand their viewpoint. Strategic leaders can gather various insights, ideas, and opinions by actively listening to diverse perspectives. This allows them to consider multiple angles and potential solutions, leading to more comprehensive and well-rounded choices.

Uncovering Valuable Information. Active listening helps executives to extract valuable information from conversations. By listening carefully and asking relevant questions, strategic leaders can delve deeper into the subject matter, uncovering important details, data, and context. This information provides a solid foundation for decision-making, ensuring that decisions are based on accurate and relevant information.

Identifying Potential Challenges and Risks. Active listening allows strategic leaders to identify potential challenges, risks, and concerns related to a decision. By actively engaging with others and listening to their perspectives, executives can uncover potential pitfalls, blind spots, or unintended consequences they may not have considered. This enables them to address these issues and make more informed decisions proactively.

Building Consensus and Collaboration. Active listening promotes collaboration and consensus-building among team members. By listening attentively to other's input, ideas, and concerns, executives can engage in meaningful dialogue and facilitate a sense of ownership and involvement. This collaborative approach fosters a shared understanding and collective commitment to the decision, leading to increased buy-in and successful implementation.

Mitigating Biases and Assumptions. Active listening helps strategic leaders overcome their own biases and assumptions. By actively seeking to understand the perspectives of others, executives can challenge their preconceived notions and consider alternative viewpoints. This helps mitigate cognitive biases' influence and allows for more objective and rational decision-making.

Enhancing Problem-Solving Abilities. Active listening facilitates a deeper understanding of problems and challenges. By actively listening to the concerns, experiences, and ideas of others, strategic leaders can gain valuable insights into the root causes of issues and identify alternative solutions. This enhances their problem-solving abilities and enables them to make decisions that effectively address the underlying challenges.

By practicing active listening, strategic leaders harness the power of diverse perspectives, gain valuable information, and facilitate collaborative decision-making, leading to improved decision outcomes and greater success in their leadership roles.

Behaviors of a Highly Effective Active, Empathetic Listener. When strategic leaders listen fully, they demonstrate key behaviors. These behaviors promote a mindset of listening more than thinking. How well do you, as a strategic leader, do this?

Assess the frequency you demonstrate the following "listen more than talk" behaviors.	Rarely	Sometimes	Always
Listen fully by eliminating distractions or declaring to the listener that now is not the time for your full attention.			
Ask questions that bring out additional perspectives and insights.			
Focus fully on the individual speaking without interrupting or providing comments.			
Acknowledge the other's views and expressions without applying your own judgement to them.			
Try, as far as possible, to understand other's views, perspectives, and feelings.			
Respond appropriately after considering what has been said.			
Give recognition to others as they have the right to speak and be treated with respect.			
Set the tone or purpose of the meeting, and then allow others to explore the issue or make recommendations.			

Note: Scholars agree that "appropriate" does not necessarily mean agreement or acceptance of what is said or requested.[3]

To be a highly effective strategic leader, fully engaging in listening promotes trust from others and demonstrates your personal empathy.

NOTHING GETS IN THE WAY OF LISTENING
MORE THAN TALKING

It's hard to listen when there is so much talking going on. Consider the following from wordsrated.com. The average person speaks around 16,000 words a day. People speak around 941 words per hour on a typical workday and spend almost two hours per day speaking. Only 5% of the words people use during the day are unique, with all others repeated. The average person uses between 2.67% and 3.35% of their vocabulary every day.[10]

Several factors contribute to the challenge for strategic leaders to listen more than talk.

Time constraints. Strategic leaders have busy schedules and numerous responsibilities, leaving limited time for listening. They may believe that because of these highly filled calendars, it's more efficient to tell and explain than to ask and listen. Telling doesn't develop relationships or allow for the deep reflection required from strategic leaders to foster innovation and solve complex problems.

Pressure to demonstrate expertise. Strategic leaders are expected to be knowledgeable and provide guidance and answers. This pressure to showcase their expertise can lead to dominating conversations and focusing on talking rather than listening.

Hierarchical dynamics. In many organizations, there is a hierarchical structure where executives hold authority. This can create a culture where subordinates are hesitant to speak up or share their opinions openly, or, as one executive pointed out to me, they are not encouraged to speak up because they do not hold the same clout as their boss. Strategic leaders are expected to demonstrate executive presence and the ability to influence, inspire, and align others with a shared vision and goals. Many strategic leaders believe this presence requires them to lead from the front, demonstrating knowledge, wisdom, and action. With a talking rather than listening mindset, strategic leaders may find it challenging to create an environment that encourages open dialogue and active listening imposed by the organisation or themselves.

Fill the void. At times, managers or individual contributors do not have the skills or confidence to speak up and lead, requiring strategic leaders to fill the gap by providing perspective, insight, and direction. Often, strategic leaders wonder why these individuals are in their roles if they can't occasionally step up to strategic challenges. Strategic leaders are then required to fill the void, and the conversation is directed back to them rather than others.

Perceived urgency. Executives make important decisions and provide direction. This can create a sense of urgency to share their thoughts and ideas. The perceived need for quick action can overshadow the importance of listening to diverse perspectives and gathering input from others.

Lack of self-awareness. Some strategic leaders may not be fully aware of the benefits of active listening. They may underestimate the value of listening to others and its impact on building relationships, fostering innovation, and gaining a deeper understanding of the organization and its employees.

Addressing these factors requires a conscious effort from strategic leaders to prioritize listening, create a culture of open communication, and recognize the importance of diverse perspectives and input from others.

DEVELOPING YOUR LISTENING MINDSET

Multiple academic studies have been undertaken to identify how listening differs from individual to individual.[11] Just as we all have different learning or speaking styles, shared wisdom suggests that there are multiple listening styles as well.

Brink and Costigan, for example, identified four styles: task-oriented, critical listening, rational listening, and analytical listening.[11]

- **Task-oriented listening:** Focuses on efficiency and actionable outcomes.

- **Critical listening:** Emphasizes evaluating and analyzing information.

- **Relational listening:** Centers on building relationships and emotional connections.

- **Analytical listening:** Involves understanding complex information and problem-solving.

Regardless of your style or preference, your previous relationship with the content or speaker impacts how you listen. If the speaker is considered an expert on the topic, we listen one way, whereas if we consider the speaker a friend, we may find ourselves listening differently.

The mindset of listening can be improved. It takes real attention to change your habits, which leads to changing your mindset. Great listening starts with being fully present, not just physically, but with your whole being.

♟ Incorporate mental presence by directing your full mental attention to the speaker and the content of their message. Avoid letting your mind wander or thinking about other things while the person is speaking. Stay focused on the conversation at hand. Take notes to help yourself concentrate. Remove your phone from your desk or at least turn it over.

♟ Leverage emotional presence by focusing on the speaker's non-verbal communication. What feelings is the other person conveying: frustration, anger, joy, concern, elation? Be aware of that emotion. Avoid taming it, but rather use it to understand the speaker's level of commitment or worry that you can help them manage or overcome.

♟ Demonstrate physical presence by using your own non-verbal cues to indicate your attentiveness, such as maintaining eye contact, facing the speaker, and adopting an open and receptive body posture. It demonstrates that you are fully engaged in what they are saying.

♟ Engage actively in the conversation by processing the other person's information and asking clarifying or broadening questions. Use questions to broaden understanding, such as, "What if?" "How will you proceed?" or "What haven't we considered?" Show genuine interest by nodding or providing verbal affirmations.

By being fully present when listening, you create a safe and supportive environment for communication, foster deeper connections with others, and enhance the quality of your interactions. It shows respect, empathy, and a willingness to understand and connect with the speaker truly.

Regardless of our style, we can all become even stronger listeners. Dozens of books and articles have been written about increasing your listening ability: remaining focused, paying attention, avoiding judgement, etc. But these one-liners are not enough to adopt a mindset of listening more than speaking. Looking at Goleman's model of three simple listening stages can pinpoint how the listening process can broaden our listening mindset.

Listening Stage	Behaviors	Mindset
Sensing. Understanding how the other person feels and observing unspoken cues.	• Notice the person's mood: is it like their usual persona? Is it agitated, jubilant, or something else? • Attend to the tempo or pace of their speaking.	• This person has something on their mind. • I care about this individual, and they aren't their usual self. I should take time to explore what's up, even if other commitments are demanding.
Processing. Remembering what the other person said; reflecting on the other person's perspective in your own thinking.	• Listen to understand, not to respond. • Focus solely on the individual. • Pause before responding.	• This is a perspective I hadn't considered. • This person is still concerned about the issue, so I need to give them attention to what's holding them back. • What new insight can I uncover that I haven't considered yet?

Listening Stage	Behaviors	Mindset
Responding. Active involvement while the other person is speaking: making eye contact, nodding, smiling, paraphrasing, and asking relevant questions.	• Ask clarifying questions. • Summarize what you heard. • Check whether you got it right. • Avoid asking questions that start with why as they create defensiveness.	• How do I support this person's perspective even if I disagree? • What am I not seeing that they see or believe? • How do I find common ground to support our relationship?

ASK POWERFUL QUESTIONS

I believe the key to great listening is asking great questions. The model I share more often than even Being vs. Doing with executive leaders is the art of asking powerful questions. I was introduced to this framework in my coaching certification program at Learning Journeys[12].

Powerful questions expand conversations, uncover unsaid perspectives, and reveal new understandings. Powerful questions

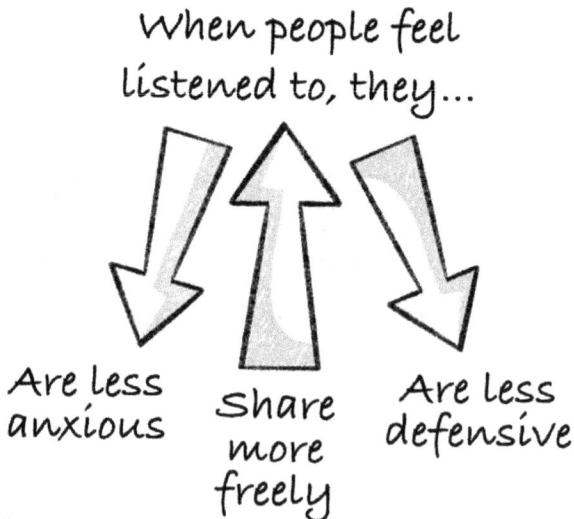

When people feel listened to, they...

Are less anxious

Share more freely

Are less defensive

never start with the word "why." "*Why*" creates defensiveness and focuses on the past: "Why do you feel that way?" "Why did that happen?" "Why isn't it finished?" It puts the hearer on the defensive, feeling they need to justify their actions.

Instead, powerful questions start with exploratory words, such as what, when, or how: "How do you plan to proceed?" "What else have you considered?" "When might I hear about the next steps?" While these are open-ended questions, they allow the topic to be explored and our collective thinking expanded.

Below are some of my favorite powerful coaching questions. Consider adding any to your listening repertoire.

- Who else should be involved that you haven't yet been able to engage?

- What haven't we considered that we should?

- What might be the best possible outcome?

- What did you learn? How will you use this knowledge in the future?

- What changes would you make if you were given a second chance?

- What would help you do better next time?

- How might I help bring this project to completion?

Notice how these powerful questions encourage conversation and not an argument. Can't remember to use them often enough? Many coaching clients place a simple Post-it not near their computer that just says: Not: Why Instead: How . . . What . . . When . . .

SO, WHEN DO YOU SPEAK?

Listening more than talking might be as much as 70% of the time. But when and under what circumstances do you speak?

Setting expectations. Leaders set direction for others to follow. In most organizations, annual or quarterly sales, quality, or profitability goals are set. Highly successful strategic leaders use these objectives to add "color commentary" to describe how overall goals connect to their individual work. Strategic leaders use their voices to explain how the work of their own team fits into the broader organizational objectives and to describe parameters that need to be met intermittently to achieve overall goals.

Providing guidance and clarification. Closely aligned to setting expectations is providing guidance and clarification. When I think about providing guidance, I often harken back to my Marine Corps days and the Five Paragraph Order. The Five Paragraph Order was a battle plan, from battalion to fire team, that outlined the mission, what had to be accomplished, when, and what supporting elements or logistics were available to help accomplish the mission. Key to these plans was the commander's intent, which provided a broader view of how the unit, say a squad, fit into the larger mission. So, if the squad's immediate objective is unachievable for some reason, such as the bridge they were supposed to cross has been destroyed, the squad leader can improvise to achieve his squad's objectives to support the overall mission.

Leaders answer questions their employees may ask, but when they do so, they offer insights from a greater perspective. An example of an answer to an employee may be: "We're installing a new enterprise resource planning system in order to automate business processes and enhance data visibility and accuracy." Now, that worker is equipped to explain what that means for the slice of the organization he manages. This guidance provides the guardrails that allow subordinates to make critical decisions and recommendations throughout the project or initiative.

Summarizing. Strategic leaders should spend a good deal of their "talking time" summarizing: "Here's what I heard; did I hear it correctly?" "What did I miss?" Summarizing, as I stated earlier, without justifying, allows the speaker or the entire room to understand the executive's perspectives and concerns about an issue further.

Expressing appreciation and gratitude. Strategic leaders, and most people leaders for that matter, don't recognize and say thank you often enough. Over my career, I've seen dozens of employee engagement surveys across both large and small organizations. The common lowest score? "I receive recognition for a job well done." As I discussed thoroughly in The 7 Mistakes New Managers Make, great recognition is not simply "good job" or "you knocked it out of the park." Highly effective recognition is specific, describing what the person specifically did that was effective and the impact that behavior had on others. It only takes a few minutes to do, yet it can have a profound effect.

Sharing important information. We've all seen it. Someone in corporate sends out a communication to executives, which gets forwarded down and down with minimal explanation or opportunities to ask clarifying questions. Sharing information is a great opportunity for strategic leaders to not only inform their leaders and teams what's going on but, more importantly, share the background and implications. Taking the opportunity to explain the decision, ask questions, and facilitate discussion demonstrates command of the organizational direction, as well as support for team members getting on board the bus to support the initiative.

There are countless opportunities for strategic executives to speak and share insights. The key mindset, however, is to be brief and allow questions to emerge from team members rather than telling them what you think they need to know. Keep in mind that strategic leaders are well ahead of the knowledge curve when it comes to organizational decisions and new initiatives. They, along with other senior executives, have been contemplating investments or initiatives often months before announcing a decision. Others don't have all the details and insights that executives have processed over time. Taking time to describe the decision and share the background that led to the decision or investment helps build support and connection for the decision.

Great listening takes time. Using powerful questions reveals perspectives that might not have been considered in the past. Focusing only on one individual or a single conversation may feel inefficient in our all-too-busy world. Yet, highly effective listeners always win the day because they show that others around them matter.

A BIT ABOUT HABITS

Throughout this chapter, I have built the case that good listening is essential and outlined ways you can improve your listening communication with others. Yes, focus on the speaker, put away distractions, and summarize what you heard without judgement. If you're like many leaders I have worked with, you've tried to become a better listener. You've created a reminder post it, yet your day-to-day challenges consistently find you telling more than asking. Perhaps it hasn't yet become a habit.

According to one study conducted by Phillippa Lally and her colleagues at University College London, it takes an average of 66 days for a new behavior to become automatic and form a habit.[13] It's important to note, however, that the time required to form a habit can vary depending on the individual and the complexity of the behavior. Lally's research showed that the range for habit formation was anywhere from 18 to 254 days. In any event, it takes time and persistence to form a habit.

The Power of Habit, by Charles Duhigg[14], explores the science behind habit forming and provides valuable insights into how habits come into being and how we can change them. Duhigg introduces the concept of the habit loop, which consists of three components: the cue, the routine, and the reward. He explains that understanding this loop is essential for understanding and changing habits. He encourages individuals trying to build or change a habit to identify *keystone* habits, which are certain habits that have the power to transform other areas of our lives. By focusing on changing these keystone habits, we can create positive ripple effects and make significant changes.

He further explains that to change habits, we have to identify the cues and rewards associated with a habit and replace them with routines that will lead to a different and desirable outcome. He reminds us to celebrate and recognize small wins. He explains that breaking down big goals into smaller, achievable tasks and celebrating small wins can build momentum and increase our chances of success.

Here's an example. Let's say you have committed to exercising more. You've bought the gym membership and the right workout shoes. Yet, every morning, you get up, get distracted, don't put on those workout shoes, and take your shower instead of going to the gym. I knew one senior executive, a mother of three, who could only work out at 6:00 in the morning based on her daily demands. She got into the habit of pressing snooze two or three times, finally getting up and searching for something to wear to the gym. Most mornings, these subtle delays prevented her from getting in her workout. She discovered that if she wore her gym clothes to bed at night and put her shoes beside her bed right in the place where she would step out of bed in the morning, half the battle was won.

Forming a listening habit can occur the same way. Come to a meeting with your powerful questions listed on a Post-it note. Commit to not being the first to speak; when you do, ask a question rather than state a perspective. Celebrate what you learned by listening instead of speaking. Remember that not every interaction will be brilliant, but if you focus on just one habit first, putting everything down and facing the individual speaking, for example, you will build your listening muscle and develop a listen-more-than-speak mindset.

ENHANCING A MINDSET FOR LISTENING

Julian Treasure is a top-rated international speaker on sound and critical listening and speaking communication skills. His Ted Talk, viewed nearly 12 million times since it first aired in 2011, offers five simple ways to improve your listening skills. Pick one and try it for a week. Then, reflect on how your day-to-day interactions have improved.[15]

Silence. Give yourself three minutes of silence each day to reset your ears. While he agrees that absolute silence is unnecessary, he encourages you to "go for quiet." His research has found that resetting your ears just three minutes a day helps clear your ears and mind from all the sounds you heard yesterday and prepare yourself for the sounds to come.

Engage the mixer. Engage with the ongoing sounds and interactions that aren't directed at you but are all around: the rhythms of the machinery operating your home or coffee shop, the traffic going by, and the conversations in their high and low tones all around but not directed at you. How many channels of sound do I hear? Julian argues that it improves the quality of your listening. I tried this recently, just before a performance by Rachmaninoff by the Tucson Orchestra. I closed my eyes and prepared for what I knew would be a special performance: violins tuning, timpani practicing their rolls, people finding their seats, and women gossiping about their trip to the venue. The hall was filled with anticipation. I was filled with joy in preparation for the concert, listening to nothing and everything all at the same time, in a way I hadn't experienced in the past from simply reading the program notes.

Savoring. Enjoy mundane sounds. Focus on a simple sound in your home: the clothes dryer tumbling, the coffee steaming machine. Challenge yourself to find the hidden choir that is all around you. And then enjoy. Enjoy the rhythm, the repetition, and the comfort of the steady, recurring sound.

Change your listening position. Become conscious of how you are positioned to listen. Not every interaction requires the same degree of attention and focus. Does a listening opportunity require active or passive listening, critical or empathetic listening, or reductive or expansive listening? Watch TV, listen to a podcast, and adopt a casual posture. Listen to the boss give you direction; focus more intently. Adopt RASA, Julian encourages. The Sanskrit word for juice, Julian turned it into a useful acronym: Receive, Appreciate, Summarize, and then Ask questions.

He encourages us to live and listen, which connects us to the speaker and the greater world around us.

A poem about listening from our ChatGPT friend.

In a world of noise and constant haste,
Active listening becomes a delicate art.
Amidst the chaos, the attention we must taste
To truly connect, we must play our part.

Distractions abound, demanding our gaze,
Technology's allure, a siren's call.

But to truly understand, we must erase
The noise that prevents us from hearing it all.

In conversations, we often wait.
For our turn to speak, to share our view.
But active listening, we must cultivate
To truly grasp the meaning, old and new.

So, let us strive to silence the noise
And listen with intent to truly understand.
For in active listening, we find the joys
Of connection, empathy, and a helping hand.[16]

PUTTING IT INTO ACTION

What **one** habit or practice would you like to adopt to advance your listening more than talking mindset?	What are you willing to **give up** to adopt this practice?

REFERENCES

1. Itzchakov, G. & Kluger, A. N. (2018) The power of listening in helping people change. Harvard Business Review chrome-extension://efaidnbmnnnibpcajpcglclefindmkaj/https://www.redpointconsulting.co.za/wp-content/uploads/2018/10/The-Power-of-Listening-in-Helping-People-Change.pdf.

2. Lee, D. & Hatesohl, D. (1993). Listening: Our most used communication skill. CM – Communications (MU Extension); 0150 (1993). https://mospace.umsystem.edu/xmlui/handle/10355/50293.

3. Macnamara, J. (2016). Organizational listening: Addressing a major gap in public relations theory and practice. Journal of Public Relations Research, 28:3-4, 146-169.

4. Lee, D. & Hatesohl, D. (1993). Listening: Our most used communication skill. CM – Communications (MU Extension); 0150 (1993). https://mospace.umsystem.edu/xmlui/handle/10355/50293.

5. Hargie, O. & Dickson, D. (2004). Skilled Interpersonal Communication: Research, Theory, and Practice, 4thed. Routledge.

6. Lindner, J. (Dec. 20, 2023). Listening Statistics: Market report & data. Gitnux.com. https://gitnux.org/listening-statistics/

7. Goleman, G. (2006). *Emotional Intelligence: Why It Can Matter More Than IQ.* Bantam.

8. Salovey, P., & Mayer, J. D. (1990). Emotional intelligence. Imagination, Cognition and Personality, 9(3), 185-211.

9. Goleman, G. (2019, July 9). Listen with mindfulness. LinkedIn.com. https://www.linkedin.com/pulse/listen-mindfulness-daniel-goleman/

10. Wordsrated.com (2023, November 13). How fast does the average person speak? https://wordsrated.com/how-fast-does-the-average-peson-speak/

11. Bodie, G. (2011, July-Aug). Conceptualization and evidence of validity within the interpersonal domain. *Communication Quarterly.* 59(3), 277–295. Bodie, G. D., Worthington, D. L., & Gearhart, C. G. (2013). The Revised Listening Styles Profile (LSP-R):

Development and validation. Communication Quarterly, 61, 72–90; Brink, K. E., & Costagan, R. D. (2023). Development of listening competence in business education. *Current Opinion in Psychology*. 04(50). 101581; Watson, K. W., Barker, L. L, & Weaver, J. B., III. (1995). The listening styles profile (LSP–16): Development and validation of an instrument to assess four listening styles. *International Journal of Listening*, 9, 1–13.

12. https://www.learningjourneys.net/

13. Lally, P., van Jaarsveld, C. H. M., Potts, H. W. W., & Wardle, J. (2009). How are habits formed: Modelling habit formation in the real world. European Journal of Social Psychology, 40(6), 998–1009.

14. Duhigg, C. (2012). The power of habit: Why we do what we do in life and business. Random House, Inc.

15. Treasure, J. (2011). 5 ways to listen better. Ted.com. https://www.ted.com/talks/julian_treasure_5_ways_to_listen_better

16. ChatOn. (2024, March 22). *GPT-40* (Chat GPT AI) . https://chat.chaton.ai/

CHAPTER 5

Take Decisive People Actions

Let's face it: all leaders have underperformers, yet not all underperformers need to be exited from their jobs or the organization. When I have debriefed with a strategic leader on a problematic performance issue that finally resolved itself, I often hear, "I wish I had taken this action much sooner." This happens, I believe, because of a leader's humanity.

There are, however, contributing factors. Harriett Porter, a long-time HR leader and talent strategy consultant with some of the largest consulting firms in the world, offers great insight. "Quite simply, organizations are afraid of getting sued."[1] America is a highly litigious society, Harriett reminded me. The U.S. has well-defined employment laws about discrimination and due process; organizations are concerned about the financial impact a termination decision may have on them. And while U.S. employment laws seem onerous, individual countries worldwide have equally strict laws to support workers. Some require months of documentation and may even require the employer to provide six months of severance when terminated.

Consider the following. Organizations seem to approach every termination as a high-risk situation, resulting most likely in litigation. The data from the Equal Employment Opportunity

Commission (EEOC) makes a compelling case for taking thorough and, at times, lengthy steps to prevent an employee from taking action against their former organization.[2]

- The average cost for an organization to defend against a single-employee lawsuit is $160,000.

- The median award for an employee plaintiff in a wrongful termination lawsuit is $70,000.

- The average length of an employment lawsuit is 18 days.

- Approximately 84% of employment discrimination cases are resolved through voluntary measures.

- Companies lose 67% of lawsuits brought against them by employees when they reach trial.

Yet, the Chief Human Resources Officers I have talked to over the years have found that most employees don't sue. They are frustrated, disappointed, and even shocked by their termination, but most often do not take action. There are

Yeah, boss, I'll get right to it.

many reasons for this. First, the employee doesn't generally understand the process for filing a grievance against their former organization. They need to hire an employment lawyer or file with the EEOC, either of whom might conclude that the employee has not been wronged. Labor law is a specialized field; law firms are highly unlikely to take an employee's case if they already represent the employer.

Former employees often "start high" with their requests only to settle; if they do so, they settle with a much smaller amount than they had hoped for. "It's hard for an employee to win a suit," said Harriett. It's financially intense for the individual to litigate the case, and individuals don't have the resources or understanding of what must happen. Most organizations negotiate solutions rather than proceeding to trial, which could take as long as a year. They have a "people first" mentality and don't want an employee case to be splashed across the headlines of their local paper or social media sites. An employee who must now spend time finding another job has little time to take action against their former organization.

WHY IT MATTERS

Let's face it: taking decisive people's action is not just avoiding a payout settlement to a departing employee. It's about your reputation. Employees notice when their bosses let bad behavior slide. They know when an employee can let deadlines slip or make inappropriate comments. While employee disciplinary actions are highly confidential, you don't share. For example, when an employee is on an improvement plan, others see your inaction as a ding against your character and leadership. Lack of action may also cause a chain reaction. "If Sharon can get away with it, so can I," allowing the entire team to lose its edge and commitment to excellence. Action on your part may prevent similar issues from others in the future because they understand the standard and what's expected.

IT TAKES COURAGE

So, if it's a regimented process to take action on a former employer, why are senior leaders so reluctant to take decisive action on underperforming employees, and what is the strategic leader mindset required to take appropriate action? Yes, executive leaders have more leverage on terminations than lower-level managers, but like any leader, they know the individual they are considering for termination. They most likely understand their family situations and outside commitments and often like the person. As a first lieutenant, I recall having a performance issue. A gunnery sergeant with fifteen years in the Marine Corps once worked for me. He was a capable administrative chief and also an alcoholic. Marine Corps performance reviews, called "fitness reports," are completed every six months on staff non-commissioned officers and officers. There is also a requirement to take and pass a physical fitness test every six months. He had been training for this fitness test for several weeks and could pass it. However, he went out drinking the night before and failed the test, walking most of the required miles. I was not only disappointed but also angry. I confronted him later about the poor performance. He promised to "stop drinking," and I gave him a lower score on his upcoming fitness report. My markings would limit his future promotion potential. It was a difficult decision to make, yet he was not demonstrating leadership for his junior Marines. It was a tough decision because I knew Gunnery Sergeant Smith well. I liked him. In most areas, he was a knowledgeable performer. Yet, he wasn't performing in every aspect of his role.

Taking decisive people's actions takes courage. We know and work with these individuals; they have performed well in some parts of their job in the past. Yet, a strategic leader's mindset considers not just the individual's impact but also the individual's impact on the broader team. Other employees see the poor performance of an individual as clearly as their leaders. They are disappointed when poor performers are "allowed to get away with not performing." Their low performance impacts others who may have to do extra work to compensate for them. A strategic leader's mindset requires them to understand the performance issue at hand and, more importantly, the impact that performance has on others.

Strategic leaders may also be reluctant to take decisive people's actions because they don't want to engage in the tedious documentation that human resources require. The leader may hit their tipping point, which is the final action by the employees that causes them to act. Yet, the leader has not created documentation over the last several months outlining how and when the employee has not measured up.

I spoke with Peter McDonald, consultant for small and mid-sized companies, working primarily with the CEO and senior leadership team. He said that he didn't struggle with taking decisive people's actions in the second half of his career. He reminded me that "you only make that mistake once." Sure, he explained that there is always hesitancy in terminating an employee, which disrupts everyone. He shared an experience of when he was a manager.

He discovered dysfunction in a team he was asked to lead; he discovered the dysfunction often harkened back to a single person. He knew he had to have a complicated conversation about his lack of performance with the individual. "Yet, when I reflected on the conversation the night before, I realized I had a role in the dysfunction. Even though this was an existing team that had been in place for many months, I didn't take the time to set expectations for each team member or the team." He told me he spent the following week defining operating principles for the team and meeting with each individual, not just the poor performer, to establish what was expected. He created a performance improvement plan and met weekly with the employee; in 0 days, the plan was completed, and the employee performed to the standard going forward.

Behaviors of Highly Effective Leaders Who Take Decisive People Actions. When strategic leaders take decisive people action, they demonstrate key behaviors. These behaviors promote a mindset of ensuring all team members are performing as expected and doing more than is expected to support the organization's mission. How well do you, as a strategic leader, do this?

Assess the frequency with which you demonstrate the following "decisive people actions."	Rarely	Sometimes	Always
Set performance expectations with each direct report, even when you are new to an existing team.			
Ensure your direct reports set clear performance expectations with each of their direct reports.			
Monitor performance by holding consistent 1:1s discussing more than just project status.			
Actively listen to employees' concerns, summarize what you heard, and allow employees to offer resolution alternatives.			
Share information with direct reports to help them understand what may be upcoming that will require their focus.			
Maintain and communicate competencies and values that can be used to set expectations and provide feedback.			
Communicate regularly with all staff. Include recognition, milestones, and initiatives that may be upcoming.			
Gather feedback about their performance and share the good and the bad with the employee.			

Assess the frequency with which you demonstrate the following "decisive people actions."	Rarely	Sometimes	Always
Document substandard performance as soon as it occurs rather than waiting for it to worsen.			

WHAT GOOD LOOKS LIKE

Taking decisive people action entails making deliberate and confident choices impacting individuals and groups. It requires a mindset that says the team is limited with this employee in place, AND this employee is most likely unhappy and performing poorly. It involves actively engaging with people, understanding their needs, and taking appropriate steps to address them.

This should include:

Setting clear goals and expectations. Clearly define the objectives and outcomes you want the individual to achieve. Identify clear measures of success and timelines. Commit these expectations to write for each direct report and ensure the copy is shared and referenced at least quarterly.

Whether team or individual goals are the *what* of performance, the skills or competencies are how the work gets accomplished. To perform well, employees need to have the skills to perform the job. A competency model, a framework for defining the skill and knowledge requirements of that job, is useful in defining job expectations. They define successful job performance.

Whether developing technical skills, such as completing month-end financial closure, running test scripts, or broadening interpersonal skills, such as collaborating or problem solving, strategic leaders find opportunities for their team to develop skills on the Joe through traditional formal learning programs.

Demonstrating open communication and collaboration. Engage in open and transparent communication with the individual and team. Clearly identify what's going well and where challenges continue. Document each discussion! Remember, all this documentation doesn't lead to a performance improvement plan or a termination. But you are prepared for quick action should the unacceptable performance not improve.

Showing empathy and understanding. Our lives are complicated: spouses lose their jobs, kids struggle in school, ageing parents are unsettled, and challenges exist with co-workers. Substandard performance may not stem from the job at all but results from the employee's life outside of work. Consider the perspectives, feelings, and concerns of the employee. It isn't your job to solve these challenges, although connecting them to resources may help. Demonstrating empathy will allow you to make decisions that are sensitive to other's needs and circumstances. Given some of the outside-of-work challenges this individual may be experiencing, you could provide access to the organization's Employee Assistance Program, usually free to employees, or extended time off, which could fall under the Americans with Disabilities Act.

Taking responsibility. As Peter McDonald explained in his interview, much of this situation could be your fault. Setting clear expectations that include both quality and timeliness measures, tracking results, and not allowing the situation to go unchecked are the strategic leader's responsibilities. Take ownership of your team's actions and their impact on others. Be accountable for the positive and negative outcomes, and be willing to adjust or course correct when necessary.

Implementing and evaluating. Follow your plans and execute the steps to bring about the desired change. Regularly assess and evaluate the impact of your actions, seeking feedback and adjusting as needed.

By taking decisive people's actions, you demonstrate proactive leadership, foster positive relationships, and create an environment that promotes growth, collaboration, and success.

TERMINATE OR DEVELOP

Substandard performance does not always end in termination. After all, the employee in question is an asset; they know the organization, know the job and have relationships with co-workers, suppliers, or customers. Terminating a poor performer can cause uncertainty among the remaining team members. People wonder, "Who will be next?" They reflect on the individual's performance and conclude, "It wasn't that bad." Finally, terminating someone leaves a hole in the team that must be filled by already fully committed colleagues or through the arduous hiring process.

As such, there are several helpful strategies leaders can deploy to help the employee return to full and effective employment.

SKILL WILL MATRIX

I often hear leaders ask, "Does the individual not know how to do the task or assignment, or are they just *not interested* in performing it?

The Skill/Will construct is a tool I often introduce to leaders across all levels of the organization. It helps a leader think not only about capability but also about an employee's motivation. A trusted tool that helps leaders reflect more deeply about an employee's capabilities, it was first introduced by Max Lundberg in his book, The Tao of Coaching, originally published in 1966 and republished in 2015[4]. The Skill/Will Matrix helps a leader think about not only capability but also employee motivation.

See the diagram at right. Leaders consider two dimensions.

♟ **Will** is on the horizontal axis. Is the person motivated to do the work? Is the work interesting and engaging for them? Are they interested or willing to perform the assigned task or project?

♟ **Skill** is on the vertical axis: Does the person have the necessary capabilities or know-how to do the job? Do they need to acquire additional knowledge or skills to accomplish the task?

HIGH	
Motivate • Learn about key motivators • Match with work opportunities • Remove constraints • Provide positive feedback	**Stretch** • Find work to delegate • Involve in larger projects • Assign to leadership roles • Make joint decisions
Direct • Set clear expectations • Teach fundmental skills • Review progress frequently • Give regular, constructive feedback • Reward positive behaviors with positive recogition	**Advise** • Teach and train • Provide close guidance and support • Give regular, constructive feedback • Clearly highlight strengths and areas to improve

Skill (vertical axis)

LOW ←———————————→ HIGH
Will

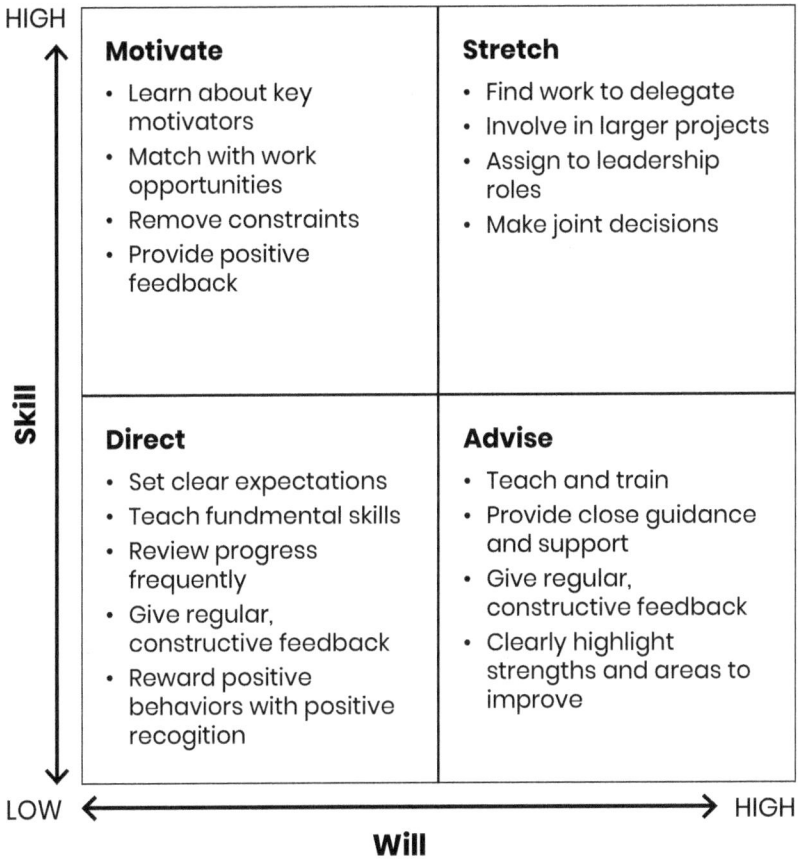

Depending on how these questions are answered, the employee will fall into one or more quadrants on the grid based on individual tasks or goals that need to be accomplished. Coaching or development is needed for each quadrant. Consider the following strategies for developing individuals based on their location on the grid.

♟ **Low Skill / Low Will.** This individual may not be worth the effort. Set clear expectations for a given timeline and then see what happens. Ensure they are properly trained for the work they are expected to deliver. Check-in regularly to discuss progress and give recognition and constructive feedback.

♟ **High Skill / Low Will:** Find out what's going on. Is the person bored? Struggling with a newly assigned task and won't ask for help? Take time to share your observations. This individual may not be aware that their motivation has changed. Reestablish expectations and find out what will re-engage them. Would they like to teach others? Take on a different role?

♟ **High Will / Low Skill:** Find more of these individuals! They are eager and willing to learn. Identify what interests them and ascertain their learning style. Consider pairing them with a High Skill/Low Will individual to learn and grow. As they learn, highlight their successes and provide corrective feedback, if necessary, so they won't develop bad habits or incorrectly learn a new skill.

♟ **High Skill / High Will:** Delegate, but don't dump. Identify things they do well and share interesting work with them. Challenge them with new learning or skills but interact with them regularly so they don't feel forgotten.

Provide honest and direct feedback. Even though you have provided feedback in a recent performance review, be-low-standard performance must be addressed with the individual head-on. Articulate in writing not only the problematic behaviors, but also outline what good looks like and when it needs to be achieved.

Provide coaching. Coaching is an investment in an individual in terms of both cost and time. Yet, I've worked with many senior leaders who have blind spots that are limiting their growth and credibility and are often unaware of how their behaviors are impacting others. Quite simply, I've worked with many of these leaders who discover their shortcomings and work diligently to find strategies to mitigate them. As an executive coach, I have seen a significant change in senior leaders when they are willing to look at themselves critically and work to modify undesirable behaviors. Yet, it's equally important to realistically weigh whether the individual has the energy to address the behavior. Will you give the employee another chance to correct the behavior, or have you concluded that your energy and open-mindedness are spent?

Does coaching really work? A meta-analysis conducted by Theeboom et al.[5] and Jones et al.[6] reviewed over 2 highly validated coaching studies and discovered that coaching significantly positively affects performance, skills, well-being, coping, work attitudes, and goal-directed self-regulation. Their findings suggest that, with time, coaching can turn around performance.

Train them. Training is certainly a possibility. Many learning professionals use the 70/20/10 model to outline learning in the workplace context. The model, created in the 1980s by three researchers, Morgan McCall, Michael Lombardo, and Robert Eichinger[7], at the Center for Creative Leadership, is a learning and development framework that suggests a proportional breakdown of how people learn most effectively.

- 70% of training should be learning in the flow of the work setting.

- 20% of learning could occur by learning from others or shadowing someone with expertise that others do not.

- 10% of learning can come from classroom learning; it is far more effective when it occurs on site because learners are given the opportunity to learn from others in their own organization and may, in fact, develop longer-term relationships following the training.

Redesign the job. Jobs expand over time. Tasks are added, and new expectations are assumed but not necessarily written down. Employees may become overwhelmed over time but are uncomfortable admitting they need help. A strategic leader's mindset requires them to consider the totality of the job to determine whether the job can be split or responsibilities given to other departments or individuals. I suggest engaging the individual in this process. Discuss what they do well and enjoy and identify which tasks they have limited skills.

Hire right the first time. We've all been there. The job has been open for months, and we hire someone we have concerns about out of frustration or exhaustion. And then, and no surprise, the employee struggles. Get it right the first time. Be patient. Listen, if you hear an inner critic warning you about a potential candidate. Make sure you are hiring for the long-term and not just for an immediate gap.

Consider job rotation. Moving someone laterally into a different role can make a world of difference. While it's bad form to shove off your low performers to another leader, you could consider rotating your team members into different roles. Yes, technical competence is critical to making this work, but giving the individual a chance to learn new skills and see things from a different perspective may give them the motivation boost they need.

Utilize small group roundtables. A less expensive model than coaching is the small group roundtable. It can be facilitated by an executive coach or a highly experienced internal facilitator. When deploying this strategy, I enroll a group of four to six leaders, generally at the same level in the organization. They conduct reflection through assessments, such as personality (MBTI, DiSC, StrengthsFinder's) or multi-rater feedback that helps individuals and their team to understand how they prefer to interact with others. They meet monthly as a group monthly and individually with me. The group cohesion and "oh, I have that problem, too" that comes from the group work is reassuring and provides new perspectives to all small group coaching members.

Change management. Change management is its own concept, but one a strategic leader should be deeply knowledgeable in. It is your job to make the case for change by explaining it, stating the benefits and timing, and making sure all stakeholders, including your employees, know what's in it for them. Some change models suggest employees fall into three categories with respect to change: they are on board, on the fence, or dissenters. At some point dissenters are allowed to disagree, but they can't "not do" the change. Having hope for these individuals is not a plan, and it undermines all that is positive in the change.

While there are endless possibilities to address substandard performance, as a strategic leader, your mindset must move an individual from bad to better. Remember to document the steps you've taken, including the dates offered, in case you must travel the termination path.

TAKING DECISIVE PEOPLE ACTION

This is not easy stuff. Taking decisive action on a substandard performance is challenging logistically and emotionally. One senior vice president reminded me, "Even at the top of the organization, I didn't have the isolated discretion to take action on a poor performer. I had to influence decisions rather than make them. I constantly reminded myself that the organization manages talent, and HR makes the final decision.

Taking decisive people action builds your reputation. Others see bad performance; they talk about it with their colleagues, and many perceive a lack of equity because standards are not being applied equally. Poor performance issues don't get better on their own. Oftentimes, I have found that employee may not be aware their performance has slipped because their decline has been gradual and tolerated. But your employee's notice. Adopting a mindset that taking action builds your own skills and the team's overall performance will make a difference with these very sensitive and difficult issues.

Know that you do not have to make these decisions alone. Document what you have done before you are fed up. Provide options and then track progress. And when it's time, work with HR to take decisive action.

What is **one** idea you took from the chapter that you will consider next time you have a substandard performer?

REFERENCES

1. Porter, H. (2024, June 13) linkedin.com/in/harriettporter.
2. Gitnux Market Data Report (2024). Must Know Employee Lawsuit Statistics. https://gitnux.org/employee-lawsuit-statistics/.
3. Peter McDonald, linkedin.com/in/peterjmcdonald
4. Lundberg, Max (2015). The Tao of Coaching. London, England: Profile Books.
5. Theeboom, T., Beersma, B., & Van Vianen, A. E. (2014). Does coaching work? A meta-analysis on the effects of coaching on individual level outcomes in an organizational context. The Journal of Positive Psychology, 9(1), 1-18
6. Jones, R. J., Woods, S. A., & Guillaume, Y. R. (2016). The effectiveness of workplace coaching: A meta-analysis of learning and performance outcomes from coaching. Journal of Occupational and Organizational Psychology, 89(2), 249-277.
7. A brief description of the 70/20/10 learning model. https://www.trainingindustry.com/wiki/content-develop-ment/the-702010-model-for-learning-and-development/

CHAPTER 6

Outward Orientation

After working on many enterprise-wide initiatives, I assumed that most executives focus on broader perspectives and align their actions with colleagues across the organization. C-suite leaders are the ones who are fully appraised of the actions and initiatives across the organization. They meet regularly, establish or reprioritize funding for critical and strategic initiatives, and then assign sponsors and teams to carry them out.

As a consultant, I have extensive experience working on large-scale initiatives. I've implemented SAP twice, consulted as a change readiness leader, and implemented an enterprise-wide career development process and portal for an organization of more than 300,000 people. I've seen these large initiatives go well and not so well. Yet, the more I thought about this chapter, the more I discovered the proper mindset wasn't about integrating actions with the enterprise alone; it was about adopting a broader orientation beyond your own department or function. I've realized that integrated actions aren't really the mindset shift at all; instead, it's about an outward orientation needed to be a successful strategic leader. Outward orientation requires a leader to move beyond their own role and think about the broader whole, not just what's happening inside their organization but within the greater ecosystem in which the organization operates. It's thinking about the interconnections and relationships between various elements within a complex system, a process that runs across departments, or the impact an organization can and is having on their greater community and the world.

I discussed this challenge with a long-time colleague, Dan Barsness,[1] a vice president of product management at several large manufacturing firms. He reminded me that having an outward focus beyond just their own function's responsibilities may be one of the most difficult transitions a strategic leader must make. "We grow up in organizations," he said, "with too much of ourselves being concerned with whether I will reach my goals or will my department be funded more fully than yours. "Will I get more people, more headcount, than you, my peer," which leads, Dan explained, "to whether my team gets more visibility with the executive team. As strategic leaders, we are suddenly expected to collaborate and support one another to get things done across the organization rather than just in our department. It requires a real difference in thinking."

This is often new territory for strategic leaders, requiring them to collaborate rather than compete for scarce people, resources or dollars. This shows up in multi-rater 360 assessments. In fact, several studies have concluded that peers are far more critical of us than our boss or subordinates. Atwater and Waldman, Bracken et al., and Van Den Berg et al.,[2] found that peer ratings among strategic leaders tend to be lower compared to ratings within other sources, such as supervisors and subordinates. They argued that strategic leaders must constantly build cross-organization relationships before they are needed by understanding what others do and how their group is impacted by a change or recommendation.

Put another way, imagine an organization as a symphony orchestra, where each vice president represents a different section of instruments such as strings, woodwinds, brass, or

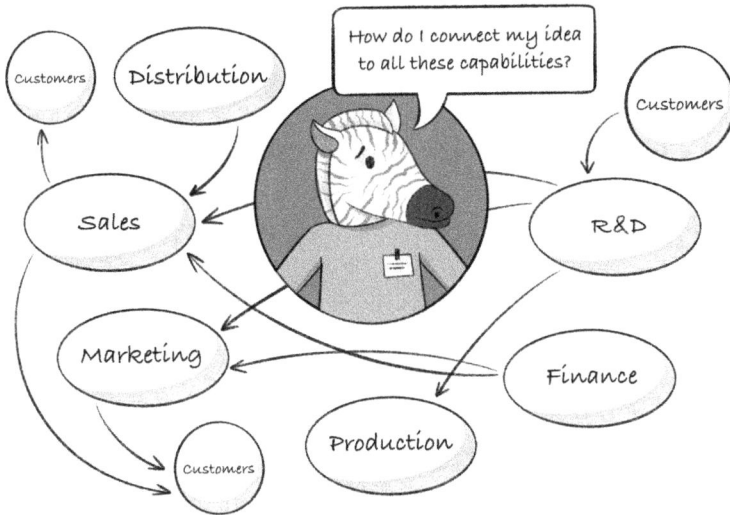

percussion, and must all work together under the guidance of the conductor to create a harmonious, unified, and brilliant performance. Similarly, vice presidents must collaborate and synchronize their actions to ensure that the organization accomplishes its goals and its broader strategic goals.

In an orchestra, musicians listen to each other, adjust their tempo, and respond to cues to create a remarkable performance.

> **Strategic leaders need to listen to each other, adapt their plans, and collaborate to address challenges and seize opportunities.**

However, a strategic leader's outward orientation doesn't stop with integrating actions within. It also includes taking time for the industry and community. I've worked with dozens of senior executives who, due to a merger or other high-impact organizational decision, find themselves without a job, often after as many as twenty years at a single organization. "My network is dried up," so many have said. It's true that they've spent so much time focusing inwardly on their organization that they haven't taken time to understand critical trends in the market or invested their own time in supporting the community. For someone who focuses outwardly extremely well, check out Kristi Fox, Executive VP at Securian's LinkedIn profile[10].

WITHIN THE ORGANIZATION

Peter McDonald[11], former vice president of corporate strategy at a major food manufacturer, stated that "not every role needs to be integrated with everyone in a large organization." If you are a P&L owner, absolutely, but other roles such as marketing and HR distribution need to be integrated, but not across the entire organization. Suppose marketing, for example, is initiating a new ad campaign. In that case, production should be made aware because they will likely see a rise in demand. Still, they don't need to be intimately involved in the planning or producing the ad campaign. There are, however, many initiatives that cross-functional boundaries. Strategic leaders must not only be aware of these initiatives but must also offer support and even resource them to ensure all aspects of the initiative have been considered. Here are a few examples.

Digital Transformation. Implementing a digital transformation initiative involves leveraging technology to streamline processes, enhance communication, and improve the enterprise's overall efficiency. Initiatives like this impact multiple functions, such as marketing, operations, finance, and customer service. Digitizing processes involves automating manual tasks and integrating systems to enable seamless collaboration and share data across the entire organization. Whether a large-scale technology transformation such as Oracle, SAP, or Netsuite, multiple functions must be engaged to ensure the new solution "works," not just for key stakeholders, finance and operations, but also upstream and downstream processes, such as sales and distribution.

Diversity and Inclusion. Fostering a diverse and inclusive work environment significantly impacts most functions within an organization. Organizations can benefit from a wider range of perspectives, increased innovation, and improved employee morale by promoting diversity in hiring practices, creating inclusive policies, and providing training on inclusive leadership. While these initiatives certainly impact functions such as human resources, talent acquisition, leadership development, and employee engagement, they also impact customer interactions, sales, and operations.

Sustainability and Corporate Social Responsibility (CSR). Implementing sustainable practices and engaging in CSR initiatives can have a far-reaching impact on an organization's operations, reputation, and stakeholder relationships. These initiatives involve reducing environmental impact, supporting community initiatives, and promoting ethical business practices. Functions such as supply chain management, operations, marketing, and public relations are directly impacted by integrating sustainability and CSR into their strategies.

These kinds of initiatives require the strategic leader to drive the whole while keeping apprised of the parts to create solutions that serve not just one's own needs or outcomes but those of adjacent, downstream, and upstream functions. Integrated or outward orientations require deep collaboration with one's peers, which is much more than knowing what their function does. It includes defining how, specifically, their function will be impacted by the initiative, requesting resources to support it to ensure their function is fully represented, and keeping abreast of developments and timelines.

Yet, doing this well requires a mindset of "this is where I should spend my time." George Murray[5], a former Army leader and strategic operations leader, reminded me. Looking back on his formidable career, George wished he had spent more time on the sales side of the business. "While you can rely on your colleagues to share key customer trends and sales challenges, it doesn't replace the 'boots on the ground' observations or a ride-along for seeing the sales process in action." Noting demands from operational issues that time and again limited his ability to spend time with the sales force, he's come to realize that understanding the challenges on the sales side more deeply would have made him a better strategic partner with his internal peers.

KEY ACTIONS FOR SUCCESSFULLY INTEGRATING ACTIONS INSIDE THE ORGANIZATION

Executive leaders I interviewed all had large scale project experiences, either as the project sponsor or program manager. They offered a number of lessons they had learned through their own experience to make these high-impact, long, and expensive projects a success.

Rally key decision makers. Key decision-makers are those whose part of the organization is directly impacted by the initiative. The leaders I spoke with encouraged you to rally these decision-makers early and often. Find out what they're excited about and discover their concerns. Then, we should engage with them regularly to find solutions so they receive what they expected when the initiative was delivered.

The CIO or CHRO can't be the sponsor. The leaders I spoke with had multiple experiences with large-scale technology or people initiatives. Let's face it, most large initiatives these days that enterprises decide to undertake have a large technology component coupled with a significant change management impact. Even diversity and inclusion initiatives will need to track engagement and resource use, requiring employees to think about things differently. New systems and processes would monitor successes and failures in attracting and re-taining diverse talent. While the technology organization plays a critical role in the success of any large initiative, executives I have spoken with agree that the CIO or the CHRO can't be the initiative's sponsor. Broad, organization-wide initiatives are intended to solve business problems, so a business leader must be the primary sponsor.

Define what good looks like. When large, organization-wide initiatives are launched, goals and measures are set, as well as timelines. Timelines and risks are reported regularly, even weekly, to the broader stakeholders. Yet, I've seen few projects consistently referring to the specific success measures established at the beginning of the initiative. Large projects naturally evolve, and the organization understands the complexities of the issues they are trying to address. This occurs even with a strong change control process. Yet, I've observed few strategic leaders who actually refer back to the success measures established early to determine whether the project is still on track. Including success measures at the top of every program status report is a best practice for maintaining this focus. When the initiative shifts, it's important for key stakeholders to ask themselves, "What does "good" look like now?"

Embrace a customer-centric orientation. Executives must prioritize understanding their customers' needs, preferences, and challenges. Yet, this is very difficult to achieve when you sit in a leadership role that is not customer-facing. I witnessed a great example through a marketing executive of a major window manufacturer, who does this exceptionally well. They were incredibly customer-intimate for both their custom-made and off-the-shelf product lines. They regularly asked for and received personalized feedback from their myriad of customers. This was achieved not only through marketing but also through sales and installers. What made this effort so impactful, however, is that her team stayed on it. They gathered this feedback month after month and then shared their insights, good and bad, with the executive team and their direct reports. I was amazed how leaders in multiple non-customer-facing departments, manufacturing, distribution, finance, etc., knew these insights almost as well as marketing. They used these insights to make business decisions. Efforts like this take time and bandwidth, yet they allow all senior leaders to make better decisions because they are focused on their customers.

Take time to build the team. When I spoke with Dan Barsness about focusing outward beyond his own function, he began not with establishing success factors or timelines; instead, he started with "knowing the team" and taking time to develop the team and manage the project. "Taking time to understand how each other "ticks" and establishing operating guidelines makes all the difference," Dan said. These simple activities are usually supported by individual and team personality assessments such as DiSC[6] or Insights Discovery[7]. He explained that he's worked on major initiatives that have done this on the front end and those who waited for a crisis to arrive and reluctantly engaged in team development. "The joy and satisfaction of working on these complex business issues was markedly different," Dan recalled. Understanding team members, what matters to them, and how they see this initiative getting across the finish line while maintaining the organization's annual performance goal changes how the initiative operates. "It makes all the difference in the world," Dan concluded.

These cross-organizational initiatives have the potential to drive positive change, improve collaboration, and contribute to the long-term success of an organization. At the strategic level, the mindset required for these initiatives is, fundamentally, "This is my job; how can I help?" Rather than "someone else has it covered." It requires reaching out to colleagues to understand how their initiative will impact your department and offer your insights and resources to support their success.

It requires a mindset shift from "I've got it covered for my group" to "How can I offer my support to ensure your success?"

OUTSIDE THE ORGANIZATION

Having an outward orientation outside the organization is equally important yet daunting challenge. The first response from nearly all leaders when asked why they aren't doing {what} more regularly is time. Yes, it does take time to cultivate external relationships, attend industry conferences, sit on non-profit boards, and influence your local government. These activities usually don't result in an immediate positive impact for yourself or your organization. The mindset shift here is understanding that time invested outside the organization will benefit both you and your organization. Consider the following.

Foster external partnerships. You don't have to go it alone. I've talked to countless executives who have been so focused on being strong financial stewards of their company's resources that it doesn't occur to them they could use external resources and partnerships to help solve their pressing issues.

Strategic leaders who actively seek out strategic partnerships with other organizations, industry associations, and trendsetters discover valuable insights, access to new markets, and collaborative opportunities. They provide industry best practices and offer the most recent research on market challenges and solutions. These relationships can be short-term, one project or a few hours of consulting, or longer-term for implementing solutions or a new business venture. They also can include coaching relationships. I have coached multiple leaders for more than three years each, all appreciating the longevity of the relationship to reflect on their growth and development over the long term.

Engage with the industry. Executives must continuously monitor and analyze industry trends, market dynamics, and emerging technologies. This can be achieved through attending conferences, participating in industry forums, subscribing to relevant publications, and engaging in continuous learning. So many executive leaders remove these from their priorities by focusing on the immediate here and now. Let's face it, we all can create clear rationales for not investing the time in attending conferences or industry forums. Again, there is no immediate impact, but the long-term insight that executive leaders can gain from engaging with one or two industry-specific organizations is immeasurable in staying abreast of their own organization and work.

Build and maintain a strong external network. Unfortunately, I'm amazed at how many senior executives have been laid off. We look at their LinkedIn profile, and it's surprising to see how little they are connected with other executives. It's common:

they have 500 or fewer connections, their profile picture is outdated, and the descriptions of their work haven't been updated in years. Further, their connections are ageing out, and they are no longer in executive roles, requiring them to start with very little in their job search. The solution to this dilemma is to keep networking throughout your career. Simon Sinek captures this concept well in his book *The Infinite Game*.[8] Sinek introduces us to the concept of an "infinite mindset" that encourages us to think more broadly about possibilities. He discusses the value of having rivals vs competitors; rivals push us to be better, while competitors are others you want to "beat." While subtle, he argues, this orientation encourages us to be much more productive in the relationships we establish and how we maintain them.

While having a substantial network is critical when a job search is imminent, developing and sustaining a professional network has numerous job-related benefits. Regularly orienting outside the organization may introduce you to new colleagues who may someday become employees. It helps you gain insights into the economic environment, regardless of the industry the colleague works in. It enables you to uncover best practices or service providers that may fit your own organization.

Sit on a non-profit board. Sitting on a non-profit board, whether it's the animal humane society or local food shelf, is eye-opening. Non-profits don't have the same level of resources that most of us have inside our own organizations. They work with minimal staff, who are often responsible for multiple areas of the organization. And yet, they make an impact: they feed the hungry, build homes for others, advocate for animals with no voice, and represent the underserved. Korn Ferry agrees. They recently covered the value of sitting on a non-profit board for your career: "Plenty of people are looking for the kind of expertise you have. Nonprofit boards always seek help with marketing, finance, technology, and other backgrounds. Board work can not only keep you professionally engaged. Still, it can also expand your network and lead to more opportunities" for you and your organization.[9]

Engage with your community. Engaging with our community is easy when our kids are in elementary or high school. It becomes much harder when we don't have that connection; they are either moved onto their own lives, or we don't have children. Politics reminds us continuously that all politics is local. This concept first emerged as early as 1932 but was made incredibly popular by Tip O'Neill, a former Speaker of the House of Representatives. Yet it's true. Change happens immediately and perhaps impactfully at the local community, even neighborhood level. To this end, I encourage you to engage locally. Join a local cause (i.e. rerouting of a key road through your community's neighborhoods) and engage in broader issues like climate change. Find a group already advocating and engage with them in letter writing or door knocking. Regularly attend city council meetings. It's a great way to meet local community members and may create future visibility for yourself.

The value of leaders engaging in activities in your local community is significant. It not only allows you to foster a sense of connection and belonging, but it also enables you to understand the needs and concerns of your community firsthand. By actively participating in community activities, you can build trust, establish strong relationships, and gain valuable insights to inform decision-making. Engaging in local community activities can inspire and motivate others to get involved, creating a positive ripple effect and fostering a sense of unity and collaboration within the community.

Behaviors of an Outward-Focused Strategic Leader. When strategic leaders orient outwardly, they demonstrate key behaviors. How well do you do this?

Assess the frequency you demonstrate the following "outward focused" behaviors.	Rarely	Sometimes	Always
Solves problems across the enterprise, connecting other functions to organization-wide solutions.			
Keeps abreast of and supports initiatives that address organizational challenges beyond just their own.			
Takes time to network outside the organization and maintains those relationships over time for personal and professional development			
Keeps abreast of industry trends by attending and presenting at trade conferences and industry seminars.			
Shares industry trends and best practices with the team.			
Considers the broader impact of the organization on society and the world.			
Supports non-profit work by joining a board of directors.			

WHAT TO LET GO OF

While senior leaders need to shift their mindsets to focus outward effectively, there are managerial skills or habits they may need to leave behind. Yet, when I ask executives about being outward-focused, they sheepishly grin and state they "don't have time." Here are a few ways of letting go you might consider.

Silo Mentality. Managers focus on their own departments or teams, working in silos without much collaboration across functions. Strategic leaders must foster a culture of collaboration and cross-functional cooperation, breaking down silos and encouraging knowledge-sharing, innovation, and collective problem-solving.

Operational Focus. Strategic leaders must avoid, as my good friend and colleague Rick Rittmaster[3] has coined, "becoming supermanagers." Managers typically primarily focus on operational efficiency and delivering results within their specific area of responsibility. On the other hand, strategic leaders must shift their focus towards broader strategic objectives, setting the direction for the entire organization. While operational excellence is still important, it should be balanced with a broader strategic and outward-looking mindset.

Tactical Decision-making. Managers frequently make decisions based on immediate needs and short-term goals. However, strategic leaders need to adopt a broader approach, delegating immediate terms to their executives, and focus instead on long-term implications, market trends, the organization's vision, and vulnerabilities. Strategic leaders should make decisions that align with the broader strategic direction, even if they do not yield immediate benefits.

Individual Performance Evaluation. Managers often evaluate and provide feedback on individual performance, focusing on day-to-day tasks and individual contributions. As senior leaders, the focus must shift towards evaluating the overall performance of teams, departments, and the organization as a whole, considering not just the goals of the organization but also market trends and best practices.

There are certainly other roadblocks to developing an outward orientation mindset; these are a few common ones. It's important to note that these skills or habits are not inherently negative, but as a leader progressing in your career, you must evolve your thinking to meet the demands of higher-level leadership positions. Two dimensions of outward focus exist: within and beyond the organization.

THE OUTWARD FOCUSED MINDSET

In the realm of leadership, a guiding light,
A leader's worth lies in their outward sight.
With a focus not on self but on their community's plight,
They inspire and empower, shining ever bright.

Amidst the chaos and the world's demands,
A leader steps outward, extending helping hands.
They listen, they learn, they truly understand,
The value of being outwardly focused; well, it's grand.

Through engagement in the local sphere,
A leader fosters unity, far and near.
They bridge the gaps, dissolve the fear,
And in their actions, hope and trust appear.

So let us celebrate leaders who hold this creed,
Whose hearts are open, whose actions lead.
For in their outward focus, great value we all heed,
A leader's impact, a community's feed[12]

Strategic leaders should invest time and effort in building relationships with influential individuals, thought leaders, and experts in their industry. This network can provide valuable advice, mentorship, and access to new opportunities. The mindset shift of being outwardly focused is simple: being out in my professional community gives me insights into my own organization and fundamentally makes me a better leader.

By adopting these strategies, executives can cultivate an outwardly focused approach that enables them to understand the external environment, anticipate market trends, and make informed decisions that drive organizational success.

Strategic leaders should invest time and effort in building relationships with influential individuals, thought leaders, and experts in their industry. This network can provide valuable advice, mentorship, and access to new opportunities. The mindset shift of being outwardly focused is simple: being out in my professional community gives me insights into my own organization and fundamentally makes me a better leader.

By adopting these strategies, executives can cultivate an outwardly focused approach that enables them to understand the external environment, anticipate market trends, and make informed decisions that drive organizational success.

PUTTING IT INTO ACTION

What is **one** habit or practice you would like to adopt to orient your outward mindset?	What are you willing to **give up** on adopting this practice?

REFERENCES

1. Barsness, D. (22 August, 2024). linkedin.com/in/danbarsness
2. Atwater and Waldman, Bracken et al., and Van Den Berg et al.[4]
3. Atwater, L. E., & Waldman, D. A. (1998). The role of peer feedback in enhancing leadership: An examination of multisource feedback. The Leadership Quarterly, 9(4), 427-448. And Bracken, D. W., Timmreck, C. W., Fleenor, J. W., & Summers, L. (2001). 360-degree feedback: A review and an evaluation framework. Human Resource Management, 40(3), 173-192.
4. Rick Rittmaster, linkedin.com/in/richardrittmaster
5. Peter McDonald, linkedin.com/in/peterjmcdonald
6. George Murray, linkedin.com/in/georgecmurray
7. DiSC. https://disctraininghub.com/purchase-disc-assessments/
8. Insights Discovery. https://discoveryourself.com/
9. This Week in Leaders. (June 27, 2024). From 'unemployable' to employable: 5 tactics. Korn Ferry. https://www.kornferry.com/insights/this-week-in-leadership/from-unemployable-to-employable-5-tactics
10. Fox, K. (2024, November 11). linkedin.com/in/-kristi-fox
11. McDonald, P. (2024, June 15). linkedin.com/in/peterjmcdonald
12. ChatOn. (2024, March 22). GPT-40 (Chat GPT AI) . https://chat.chaton.ai/

CHAPTER 7

Act Courageously

Adam Grant describes acting courageously as the willingness to act despite fear and doubt, driven by a sense of moral conviction and a desire to make a positive impact[1]. Malcolm Gladwell encourages leaders to act courageously by challenging conventional wisdom[2]. His interpretation involves perceiving risk, leveraging persistence and resilience, and acting with more courage. Maya Angelou spoke about courage as the ability to confront and overcome fear. Aristotle described it as a virtue and emphasized the importance of facing fear and acting in the face of danger or adversity. In short, acting courageously is a mindset to willingly act despite fear, uncertainty, and risk.

In the fast-paced and ever-changing business landscape, strategic leaders must be willing to embrace change, take calculated risks, and adjust their strategies as needed. Nearly everything is changing in this dynamic global economy. Results are uncertain; strategies to undertake them are even less clear. The key is not to drive ambiguity out but to become more comfortable working with what you have and acting decisively.

In this chapter, we discuss courage, courage to act when the options are unclear, and courage when both the risk and reward are significant. It's about valuing your intuition, leveraging the perspectives of others, acting, and then taking ownership of your decision. Courage clearly isn't a competency; it's a mindset. Strategic leaders are expected and required to act courageously in their roles, regardless of their role.

Korn Ferry defines courage as stepping up to address difficult issues, saying what needs to be said, and acting on what needs to be done. In their multi-year global analysis of leaders who demonstrate strong courage, they have discovered courage is more difficult to develop than other leadership capabilities. Yet, surprisingly, courage is in high supply, suggesting that highly effective executives have learned to take measured risks despite not having all the data they would like to inform their decisions.[3]

Courage, however, is complicated. It involves trusting your own experience and know-how, surrounding yourself with highly trustworthy and capable team members, displaying decisive decision-making skills, and, as Adam Grant has so aptly described in *Think Again*, overcoming the fear of not speaking up.[1]

I recently discovered and thoroughly enjoyed Robert Rubin's new book, *The Yellow Pad*.[4] Robert Rubin is a retired banking executive, lawyer, and former U.S. Secretary of the Treasury during the Clinton administration. The book fundamentally focuses on decision-making and calculating the risk associated with potential options. Rubin shared that courageous leaders don't necessarily jump immediately to action in a difficult circumstance, but they don't overly ponder their next steps either.

Rubin introduces us to an unusual speaking invitation he received from an inmate at San Quentin Penitentiary following his time at the White House.[5] He agreed to the request and spent time with several inmates to plan the focus of his talk. During the planning conversation, he recalls inmates sharing life lessons they discovered during incarceration. One profound framework he heard from one inmate and one way to think about acting courageously is what one inmate called *reacting versus responding*. The inmate, and others like him, had discovered the impact of *reacting* to a situation in a moment and the catastrophic consequences often resulting in multiple decades in prison.

Rubin explains that "to react is to make a decision based on a split-second, emotionally charged impulse; responding, on the other hand, involves thought and patience. It requires stepping back to consider the situation and the potential consequences of one's actions."[4] Reacting, another inmate explained, can have significant consequences. Twenty-eight inmates calculated the impact of their "in the moment" reactions. They estimated that their response to a situation lasted collectively for about four and a half minutes, resulting in 715 years of incarceration!

This concept of reacting vs. responding seems closely connected to acting courageously. Leaders who act courageously aren't making snap decisions in the crisis of the moment. Malcolm Gladwell encourages us to have a perception of risk and leverage persistence and resilience. Courage is not something that you already have that makes you brave when the tough times start, Gladwell argues. Courage is what you earn when you've been through tough times and you discover you've made it through them and come out with different insights on the backend. Although he doesn't say so, he clearly thinks that acting with courage is responding rather than reacting. Yes, courageous leaders can make quick, high-impact decisions but generally don't do it immediately. They pause, reflect on the situation, gather perspectives, and act, even in high-impact, high-risk situations.

WHAT ACTING COURAGEOUSLY LOOKS LIKE

Acting courageously isn't generally a single action; as highlighted above, it generally isn't a response to a single situation in a moment. Rather, strategic leaders who act courageously develop a mindset that allows them to demonstrate several behaviors that they leverage over time that allow them to act courageously when the situation demands. It's fundamentally about our principles and values. When I speak with executives who see themselves as courageous, they often harken back to their childhoods. Their courageousness, many say, was formed from a parent who encourage them to try things a different way, get out of their comfort zone, and try something, even if they don't know whether it will work.

Courageous leaders are willing to take calculated risks and step out of their comfort zone. They understand that progress and growth require stepping into the unknown and embracing uncertainty. They don't move blindly into the unknown and are not thrill seekers, but they use their experience and know how to deal with the situation they are faced with.

They make difficult decisions, even when faced with opposition or adversity. Highly effective, courageous leaders can analyze situations quickly, gather input from others, and take action for the greater good of their organization; they aren't focused on their own recognition or advancement as much as making the right decision at the right time for the good of the whole.

Courageous leaders speak up and advocate for what's right, even when others disagree. They are comfortable challenging the status quo and standing up for their own values and principles, even when their position may be unpopular and may impact their reputation.

They are adaptive and are early drivers of change. They understand that change is inevitable and necessary for growth and innovation. They inspire others to understand and embrace change and navigate inevitable obstacles.

Courageous leaders inspire and empower others. They lead by example, set high standards because they believe high standards are possible, and encourage others to pursue their own courageous actions. They create an environment where others know they will have their back if they boldly move or express their controversial perspectives. They allow their team to fail fast and then reflect on what they've learned from the experience.

They are highly resilient. Courageous leaders can gain traction, even after a failure. They utilize and maintain their energy such as exercising regularly, monitoring their eating habits, getting the right amount of sleep, and spending limited time scrolling for nonsense on their phones. They find learning and personal growth in setbacks.

RELATED CONSTRUCTS ON ACTING COURAGEOUSLY

Acting courageously is a complex idea. I've highlighted a few thought leaders who have weighed in on the value and aspects of acting courageously. Additional scholars have contributed as well. Their work has centered on exploring theories of human behavior, motivation, and leadership to articulate several well-regarded schools of thought that value forward-looking, deliberate, strategic action. Consider the following.

Rationale Decision Making. Acting courageously certainly begins with solid decision-making. Decision-making is essential in any workplace where managers, leaders, and employees must make effective decisions that will lead to positive outcomes. Decision-making can seem irrational, based immediately and from the gut, or a *reaction*, as Rubin might have coined it. U.S. political scientist and 1978 Nobel Prize Laureate Herbert Simon was one of the first theorists who introduced the importance, benefits, and process associated with effective decision-making.[6] Smith asserted that decision-making is the heart of effective leadership and that effective decision-making must be derived from the logic and psychology of human choice.

Countless models for rational decision-making exist within academic publications and the internet, for that matter. Most processes include some form of the following:

♟ Identify the ultimate goal or outcome

♟ Identify alternatives or options

♟ Evaluate options against the identified set of critical outcomes

♟ Decide and implement

So many leaders I've worked with struggle with decision-making because they see it as time-consuming and even cumbersome. They struggle to consider alternatives, particularly when the "right" decision seems obvious. Acting courageously involves thinking strategically, rather than tactically, about decisions. It's moving beyond the here and now and thinking about the impact of a decision both now and in months to come. Imagine you are playing a game of chess. Tactical decision-making, in comparison, is about the individual moves you make during the game to capture your opponent's pieces or defend your own. These tactical moves are focused on immediate opportunities and threats on the chessboard. They require quick thinking and analysis of the current situation to gain a temporary advantage. Tactical decision-making refers to the process of making decisions that are focused on achieving short-term goals and objectives. These decisions are more frequently made by middle-level or lower-level managers. They are aimed at addressing immediate operational issues or challenges.

In contrast, strategic leaders make their share of "here and now" decisions. Tactical decisions are more specific in nature and are often routine or repetitive. They are made within the framework of the organization's existing strategies. They are meant to support the implementation of those strategies.

Strategic decision-making, on the other hand, involves making long-term decisions that have a broader impact on the organization as a whole. Senior-level executives, such as the CEO or the board of directors, make strategic decisions. They are aimed at shaping the overall direction and future of the organization. These decisions are typically complex, non-routine, and often involve significant risks and uncertainties. Strategic decision-making involves analyzing the external business environment, assessing internal capabilities, and formulating strategies to position the organization for sustainable success.

In chess, strategic decision-making involves your overall game plan and long-term approach. It includes decisions about positioning your pieces, planning your attack, and anticipating your opponent's moves. Strategic decisions require a deeper understanding of the game, considering the future consequences of your moves, and adjusting your overall strategy accordingly. Tactical decision-making corresponds to the short-term moves you make during the game, while strategic decision-making relates to the overarching plan and long-term vision that guides your function or organization. In acting courageously, leaders focus on long-term outcomes versus immediate results.

WHAT GETS IN THE WAY OF GREAT DECISION-MAKING?

Of the hundreds of strategic leaders I've interacted with over my career, one stands above all others in decision-making: Tom Kingston, Executive Director of the Wilder Foundation in

St. Paul, MN[7]. Tom was an exceptional leader in many ways; the one I admired most was how he approached key decisions. Working for a major social services provider in the greater St. Paul area, the demands from those in need far outweigh the organization's ability to serve, making key decisions even more challenging. Like most executives, Tom surrounded himself with many highly capable senior leaders; most had been in the organization for years while serving the Wilder client population.

When he had a critical decision to make, perhaps it involved closing a program, reallocating funds, or experimenting with a new offering, he would clearly lay out the process for them. He valued their input and would often allow them to make decisions collectively. However, he equally outlined the situation, asking for their input but being clear initially that he would be responsible for the decision and under what timeline. When I gathered performance feedback for the Board multiple times, this clear decision-making approach was always among Tom's strongest capabilities.

Process and roles make a clear difference in effective decision-making. Yet, our own biases significantly impact our ability to make high-impact, high-quality decisions. One of the most rewarding classes I took as a graduate student was on the art and science of decision-making. Decision-making heuristics are rules of thumb we leverage based on past experiences, reason, and generalizations that we utilize to move decision-making along quickly, but can also hinder our ability to make well-thought-out, concise decisions. I don't believe we discuss these often enough. While entire graduate courses cover them, here are a few.

Anchoring and Adjustment Heuristic. We tend to rely heavily on the first piece of information encountered, the "anchor," when making decisions and adjusting from that initial reference point. Notice if you are looking for a new car, a red one, suddenly all you see are red cars on the road. You decide that is too common of color for your next purchase when the percentage of red cars on the road is only about eight or nine percent.

Confirmation Bias. We tend to seek and favor information that confirms our pre-existing beliefs or hypotheses while ignoring or discounting contradictory information. We all do this. For example, someone may believe that a particular vitamin supplement improves their immune system. They may actively seek testimonials and articles highlighting the supplement's benefits and dismissing studies that indicate that the supplement may have potential risks.

Loss Aversion Bias. We tend to have a stronger aversion to losses compared to equivalent gains. This particularly plays out in investment choices and negotiation strategies. Imagine an investor who has purchased shares of stock at $100. After some time, the stock's price drops to $70. Due to loss aversion, the investor may be reluctant to sell the shares, fearing the realization of the loss. They might hold onto the stock hoping to rebound to the original price, even if indicators suggest it may not recover.

Availability Heuristic. We tend to rely on easily accessible and vivid information when making decisions rather than considering the statistical or objective probability of events. Consider crime rates. If someone frequently watches news reports about violent crimes, they may start to believe that crime is much more common than it actually is. The vividness and frequency of these reports make such incidents readily available in one's memory. As a result, they might overestimate the likelihood of becoming a victim of crime, even if crime statistics show that overall crime rates are declining.

Overconfidence Bias. We may overestimate our own abilities, knowledge, or the accuracy of our judgments, leading to excessive confidence in our decisions. Consider a professional athlete with a few standout games and receiving praise from coaches and fans. This success may lead the player to overestimate their abilities, believing they can perform exceptionally well without needing to train as rigorously or failing to analyze their opponents' strategies, leading eventually to poorer performance when taking on more prepared opponents.

Sunk Cost Fallacy. We tend to continue investing time, money, or resources into a project or decision, even when it is no longer rational because we have already invested so much. Think of it as throwing good money after bad. Imagine a couple who has spent several years together yet unmarried. As time goes by, they realize that their relationship is no longer fulfilling, and their differences might not be able to be resolved. Yet, they own a home together and have many shared friends. They continue to endure the situation, even marry, hoping this will somehow change the situation and their perspectives.

Recency Bias. We tend to give more weight or importance to recent events or information while overlooking or underestimating long-term trends or historical data. Consider a professional baseball team. The team has a mixed record throughout the season, but in the last few games, they have achieved a series of impressive victories. As the playoffs approach, fans, analysts, and even coaches may overemphasize the recent winning streak while downplaying the team's earlier struggles. This could lead to an inflated belief in the team's chances of success in the playoffs and ignoring their poorer performance earlier in the season.

Framing Effect. This results in the tendency to be influenced by how information is presented or "framed," leading to different decisions based on how the same information is worded. An example of the framing effect can be seen in medical decision-making. Consider two patients presented with information about a surgical procedure with a certain risk of complications. The first patient is told, "This surgery has a 90% success rate;" the second is told, "This surgery has a 10% failure rate." Despite both statements conveying the same statistical information, the first patient is more likely to view the surgery favorably, while the patient in the second situation may be more hesitant or inclined to avoid the surgery due to the negative framing.

Heuristics are fascinating and can require deep exploration to fully understand. Yet, to leverage this insight in decision-making is not necessarily needed. The point is that our personal biases, based on our past experiences and confidences, impact our decision making despite the presented data, so we must be mindful of these biases and guard against them.

Learning Agility. Successful strategic leaders who act courageously are agile learners. Michael Lombardo and Robert Eichinger first defined learning agility in 2001[8]. They differentiated between learning agility, navigating your way through a new or unique situation without knowing what to do, and learning ability, which focuses on applying one's cognition and learned know-how. They were among the first researchers to suggest highly agile, flexible learning, learning from experience and then applying it to new situations, is a key measure or predictor of high potential.

Korn Ferry has described learning agility as "the willingness and ability to learn from experience and then apply those lessons to succeed in new situations. Leaders who are learning agile continuously seek new challenges, solicit direct feedback, self-reflect, and get jobs done resourcefully."[9]

Learning agility is the willingness and ability to learn from experience and subsequently apply that learning to perform successfully under new or first-time conditions. Learning agility is vague to define and even harder to articulate. It involves your willingness to learn from your experience, particularly mistakes or blunders, and then apply your learnings, not all of them, but some of them that may be relevant, to a new or unusual situation. Because of this agility, you can avoid pitfalls and apply your knowledge to unique and untried situations.

Think of learning agility as a chameleon, known for its ability to change its color and blend in with its environment, allowing it to stay hidden and protect itself from predators. Similarly, learning agility is the ability of individuals to adapt and thrive in different situations. Like a chameleon, leaders with high learning agility can quickly assess new environments, identify the key elements, and adjust their approach accordingly. They are flexible, open-minded, and willing to step out of their comfort zones. Just as a chameleon's ability to change color helps it survive and thrive in various environments, learning agility enables individuals to navigate unfamiliar challenges, acquire new knowledge and skills, and find innovative solutions.

Growth Mindset. Psychologist and Stanford University Lewis and Virginia Eaton Professor Dr. Carol Dweck has bridged her work of developmental psychology, social psychology, and personality psychology to understand how self-conceptions explain motivation, self-regulation, and personal achievement,[10] and introduced us to the concept of the *growth mindset*.

After studying the behavior of thousands of children and their willingness, or lack of willingness, to venture into new territory or try new concepts, Dr. Dweck and her colleagues coined the terms fixed mindset and growth mindset to describe people's underlying beliefs about their own learning and intelligence. When students believe they can get smarter, she discovered that they understand that effort makes them stronger, not inborn intelligence.[11] Growth mindset, therefore, is one's ability and willingness to improve through dedication, effort, and learning. Individuals with a growth mindset tend to achieve higher levels of success. They are more resilient in the face of challenges than those with a fixed mindset who believe their abilities are fixed and cannot be changed. Her groundbreaking highlighted the importance of fostering a growth mindset in individuals of all ages to unlock their future potential and promote lifelong learning.

Leaning into Risk. I shared the insights I gleaned from Robert Rubin's The Yellow Pad earlier in this chapter about his framework for reacting versus responding. In his book, Rubin introduces us to Raphel Demos, an authority on Greek philosophy and Harvard Alford Professor of Natural Religion, Moral Philosophy, and Civil Policy.[12] Rubin reflects on his introduction to philosophy class as a sophomore and "came to appreciate that any proposition to be true in the final and ultimate sense was impossible."[5]

In a New York Times Opinion piece,[13] Rubin shared his approach to decision-making he had learned, partly due to his exposure to Raphel Demos. "At the heart of my own approach is 'probabilistic thinking,' the idea that nothing is 100 percent certain and that everything is therefore a matter of probabilities." He describes how he uses a simple yellow legal pad to list possible outcomes of a simple or complex decision in one column and then his best estimates of the probability or likelihood of each occurring in the second column.

He has discovered that this approach has changed how he thinks about risk. He argues that decision-makers too often focus on a very narrow set of, often optimistic outcomes, leading them to narrow thinking and perhaps making poorer decisions. Probabilistic thinkers, as he calls them, recognize that risk includes a wide range of possibilities. By bringing probabilistic thinking into decision-making, one becomes more aware of and able to articulate the trade-offs of one decision over another.

For example, say you are presenting a somewhat controversial, but desperately needed investment in your organization's infrastructure to the board. You've done your due diligence and have a compelling case for action: the current infrastructure configuration simply will not support more capacity as the organization grows at 10 to 20% yearly. In preparation, you complete a yellow pad analysis. On the left, you list all the possible outcomes of deciding to move forward, and on the right, you list the probability of success for each.

Decision => Move forward with the infrastructure investment

Case for Action => The current infrastructure configuration simply will not support more capacity as the organization continues to grow

Possible Outcomes	Probability of Occurring
Delivered updated infrastructure within budget and on schedule.	**10%.** Everything goes right: on time and budget with no quality issues, allowing the organization to continue growing.
Delivered updated infrastructure as envisioned and on schedule but encountered unforeseen technical challenges that caused the investment to increase.	**30%.** On time, on quality, but not within budget. Delivered updated infrastructure as envisioned, on-time, and on-budget, but infrastructure needs evolved during the time of implementation (i.e., the company acquired a large competitor), and now more time, budget, and updates are needed.
Delivered on-time, on-budget, on-quality, but overlooked something important that wasn't even considered earlier in terms of needed capability.	**40%.** Delivered with some delays and organizational turnover but delivered most of the functionality needed. Also assumed to be on-budget? "Do what you can for $X, but spend no more than $Y."
Total failure due to the solution not being able to deliver what was promised, and the project needs to be started afresh.	**10%.** Edge case where everything goes wrong: not on-time, not on-budget, and not on-quality (i.e., updated infrastructure is never completed or is completely ineffective at supporting more capacity to allow the org to continue to grow).

Possible Outcomes	Probability of Occurring
Total failure not only needs to be started afresh but impacts something else that jeopardizes the stability of the business.	**5%.** Everything goes wrong, and it makes the situation even worse.

Thank you, Warren Golla[14], longtime friend, colleague, and partner at Trexin Consulting, for this insightful analysis. Over my career, I've worked with dozens of organizations that have embarked on lofty IT transformation initiatives. They've created a case for action, found a reliable integration partner, appropriately budgeted, and set off, but only months later, the program is desperately off track. Not once have I seen an organization engage in this kind of probability planning that might have fended off disaster.

This clarity allows you and all stakeholders at the top of the organization to clearly know the challenges they approach, the likelihood of them occurring, and the willingness to create contingency plans for the worst possible outcomes.

ACTING COURAGEOUSLY IN ACTION

Meet Kyra Daley,[15] a Naval Academy graduate and Naval public affairs officer. As a senior communication and media advisor to some of the Department of Defense's largest and most high-profile programs, she spent considerable time supporting flag officers (admirals) within the Pentagon, preparing them to influence their foreign counterparts or prepare for U.S. media interviews. I asked her about courage. "Courage doesn't come to you in the spur of the moment," Kyra began. She said it is developed over time, first from your upbringing and the values your parents instilled. Then, she said, these values are strengthened over time by the individuals you interact with and the organizations you work for.

She recalled a time as a senior officer new to command at the Pentagon. Shortly into her tenure, she discovered that a particular reserve flag officer was "overleveraging" the lack of enforced guidelines around travel expenses. She recalled a time when this officer included an additional four or five staff officers to accompany him to a site visit in Italy, even though the regulations clearly stated that he was only allowed a single aide on such a visit. She realized that this individual had been leveraging a lack of oversite for several years, bringing along his Navy pals on the government's dime regularly with impunity. She wondered if he hadn't been called on it in the past due either to his rank or perhaps his arrogance.

"It did take courage to address the situation," Kyra shared, although she agreed it didn't seem courageous in the moment. Kyra responded rather than reacted. She discovered that this inappropriate use of government funds had become a habit by the flag officer, ultimately limiting training resources and readiness for other command members. While there are official avenues to address this kind of abuse, Kyra exercised her courage by first researching Navy regulations to ensure the way she saw the situation was, in fact, in violation. She discussed the issue with a colleague in a supporting command to ensure she hadn't overlooked perspectives.

"He was angry," was Kyra's reaction when I asked her how the conversation went. "I was uncomfortable because he was a senior officer and had been doing this for so long. He seemed to have convinced himself that his practices were okay." But she held firm. She reminded him of the regulations and how he had violated them. He threatened to ruin her career. She didn't want to move the situation through formal channels; she just wanted his travel excesses to end so members of the command could better leverage the budget for readiness.

Adam Grant would have been proud of her. She acted with courage despite her own fear and doubt. She stood up to power because of her knowledge that the Navy regulations were on her side, and in doing so, she was positively impacting her unit.

PUTTING IT INTO ACTION

Are you acting courageously? When strategic leaders act courageously, they demonstrate a mindset for acting and a number of key behaviors that support their mindset. How well do you, as a strategic leader, do this?

Assess the frequency with which you demonstrate acting courageously	Rarely	Sometimes	Always
You make sense of complex, high-quality, and sometimes contradictory information to gain clarity and focus.			
You take charge and are comfortable directing others and accepting responsibility for decision-making.			
You explore possibilities and then turn ideas into reality; you are future-centric.			
You are situationally aware. You constantly gather immediate feedback from the situation, both positively and negatively, and adjust your approach accordingly.			
You are aware of your impact on those around you and request feedback regularly.			
You take on new opportunities and tough challenges with a sense of urgency and enthusiasm.			
You maneuver through complex policies, processes, and politics to create positive outcomes and support.			

What is **one** habit or practice you would like to adopt to advance your willingness to act courageously?	What are you willing to **give up** on adopting this practice?

REFERENCES

1. Grant, A. (2021). Think again: The power of knowing what you don't know. Viking.
2. Gladwell, M. (2000). The Tipping Point: How Little Things Can Make a Big Difference. Brown, Little.
3. Korn Ferry (2022). Korn Ferry leadership architect global competency framework, Version 14.14c. https://www.kornferry.com/products. p.1.
4. Ruben, R. (2023). The yellow pad: Making better decisions in an uncertain world. Penguin Press.
5. Ruben, Robert, (n.d.) https://tedxinprisons.fandom.com/wiki/Robert_E._Rubin.
6. Smith, A., (1947). Administrative Behavior: a Study of Decision-Making Processes in Administrative Organization McMillan.
7. The Wilder Foundation. https://www.wilder.org/
8. Lombardo, M. M., & Eichinger, R. W., (2001, January 8). High potentials as high learners. Human Resource Management: Advancing Human Resource Research and Practice. 39(4), p321-329.
9. DeMeuse, K. P. (n.d.) What's smarter than IQ? Learning Agility. It's number one above intelligence and education in predicting leadership success. Korn Ferry Institute https://www.kornferry.com/content/dam/kornferry/docs/pdfs/whats-smarter-than-iq-learning-agility.pdf.
10. Dweck, C. (n.d.). https://profiles.stanford.edu/carol-dweck
11. Dweck, C. (2006). Mindset: The new psychology of success. Random House.
12. Demos, R. (n.d.). https://en.wikipedia.org/wiki/Raphael_Demos#:~:text=Raphael%20Demos%20(%2F%CB%88d%C9%9B,of%20the%20Greek%20philosopher%20Plato.

13. Rubin, R. E. (2018, April 30). Robert E. Rubin: Philosophy prepared me for a career in finance and government. New York Times. And, Rubin, R. E. (2023, May 9). I don't have the secret to making hard decisions, but I do have a yellow note pad. New York Times. https://www.nytimes.com/2023/05/09/ opinion/hard-decision-making-uncertainty-robert-e-rubin. html?searchResultPosition=3

14. Warren Golla. linkedin.com/in/warrengolla

15. Kyra Daley. (linkedin.com/in/kyra-daley-24439b2),

CHAPTER 8

Comfort with Ambiguity

Ambiguity is a parallel element of risk-taking: what risks or decisions are you willing to make given what you don't know? I've worked with many executives over the years who believe they are risk takers but fundamentally are risk averse because they don't want to make a mistake. They may state they're "comfortable with risk. I just need to know the most likely outcome." This personal quest to *knowing* the outcome is the antithesis of risk-taking and comfort with ambiguity. While risk-taking is scary, the mindset for embracing ambiguity must be that you're not alone; you have the organization and your years of experience on your side to use your best judgment to move the organization forward.

Highly effective strategic leaders who are talented at living with ambiguity have shifted their mindset by trying *not* to drive toward clarifying the unknowns. They understand risk, welcome creativity in finding solutions, and are willing to try ideas that may not have been successful in the past.

I realized I was in the center of experiencing "comfort with ambiguity" when I facilitated a strategic planning session with a group of non-profit executives. Their organization was experiencing a dramatic industry upheaval driven by a newly created congressional requirement. Their future was uncertain, so their strategic plan was critical to their existence. In preparation for the day's executive session, I worked closely with their chief administrative officer to plan the day. We had leaders who engaged with the pre-work and were committed to the future of their mission-driven organization. The exercises we planned to use were ones I had used regularly in the past.

Yet, as the day began and we got through the opening experience, I realized the day could have fallen apart at any time. While I'd done dozens of similar workshops in the past, I knew that a single individual could derail the entire day at any moment. Someone could, for example, remind the group that the "novel" approaches they had identified had been tried before. They could have been impatient with the pace of the workshop and encouraged the group to skip critical reflection points and "cut to the chaise." An emergency within the organization could have arisen, requiring several executives to leave the session to address it. I realized I was in a sea of ambiguity!

Fortunately, none of those things happened, but I knew they could. I knew from experience that one executive team member could send the whole workshop sideways at any moment. Yet, I trusted my experience and the planning we had done. And I trusted myself. I didn't know how the workshop would end or what strategic priorities would emerge. Still, I leveraged my experience and confidence to help the leaders rest in a state of ambiguity to allow them to explore what might be for this amazing organization.

Comfort with ambiguity, I have found, is not about engineering the process or product to the last detail so nothing can possibly go wrong. It's about adopting a mindset that not knowing what could happen is okay and having the personal confidence that if it does, when it does, you have the skills, abilities and experience to deal with it and help others move forward. Uncertainty, paradox, nebulous outcomes, and ambiguity, I have discovered, are at the center of innovative thinking.

> **Comfort with ambiguity happens when leaders recognize and accept that the unknowns outweigh the knowns by a wide margin.**

Micheal Gelb[1], author and executive coach, facilitates creativity and innovation and brings breakthrough thinking to organizations. His work is heavily informed by the deep-dive research he completed on the fifteenth-century genius Leonardo da Vinci. He discovered that this painter, sculptor, engineer, scientist, and architect utilized seven principles that drove his innovative mindset and breakthrough ideas. Jacqueline Byrd[2], author, executive coach, friend, and former business partner, spent her life's work helping organizations thrive in uncertainty, understand risk, and leverage their creative potential to create breakthrough solutions. Her Creatrix assessment[3] helps people understand their propensity to take risks and be creative. Through her research, she discovered that these two dimensions, risk-taking and creativity, drive innovative thinking.

Jacqueline gathered perspectives of over 125 innovators, those who regularly inspired breakthrough thinking, and discovered seven practices they consistently leverage.

Below is a comparison of Gelb and Byrd's research. Notice the similarities between Gelb's innovative principles that da Vinci applied over five hundred years ago and those uncovered by Byrd from today's living, breathing breakthrough thinkers.

Leonardo da Vinci's Principles	Voice of the Innovator's Practices
An insatiable curious approach to life and an unrelenting quest for continuous learning.	Go outside existing resources and see the world in different ways.
Recognition of an appreciation for the interconnectedness of all things and phenomena.	Stay curious and look for interconnections between things that don't always seem to belong together.
The development of the balance between science and art, logic and imagination.	Always believe that there is a better way.
A willingness to embrace ambiguity, paradox, and uncertainty.	Believe in the freedom of thought.
A commitment to test knowledge through experience and willingness to learn from mistakes.	Stay outspoken.
The cultivation of grace, ambidexterity, fitness, and poise.	Stay determined.
The continual refinement of the senses as a means to enliven experience.	Stay confident in yourself.

WHAT COMFORT WITH AMBIGUITY LOOKS LIKE

Descriptions of comfort with ambiguity abound. Below are a few I trust most often.

- Korn Ferry's leadership architect suggests being comfortable with uncertain information and unclear situations and open to alternate solutions.[4]

- Creatrix describes it as being able to operate with uncertainty and vagueness, working without high structure, goals or objectives to accomplish or create.

Leaders who have a mindset of comfort with ambiguity:

- Suspend the need for more information. They work with the information they have rather than needing and asking for more information.

- Ask, "How might this work?" rather than "Here is the problem."

- Take time away from operational issues to gather the team to wonder and create.

- Facilitate innovative thinking by using tools other than brainstorming.

- Are decisive despite uncertainty and vagueness.

- Imagine a future without having a clear plan of how to get there.

- Can put themselves in someone else's shows and see their needs and perspectives.

- Act without the total picture.

Having a mindset of comfort with ambiguity is about being inner rather than other-directed. An other-directed orientation is guided by current trends or outward influencers rather than from within. It's listening to your inner voice and having the confidence to know that it is on track. It's dismissing the inner critic and letting the inner proponent and advocate lead the way.

Put another way, being comfortable with ambiguity is similar to a skilled chef experimenting in the kitchen. Just as a chef navigates the uncertainties of flavor combinations and cooking techniques, being comfortable with ambiguity embraces the unknown and explores new possibilities. Comfort with ambiguity suggests that you aren't always clear on the outcome but are comfortable with that occurrence. In cooking, mistakes can lead to unexpected discoveries or new recipes. A chef embraces these moments as opportunities to learn and improve. Similarly, those who are comfortable with ambiguity see challenges and setbacks as valuable experiences that contribute to personal growth.

UTILIZE BREAKTHROUGH THINKING TECHNIQUES

"But I'm not creative." I've heard it from many executives. My response is always the same: "You don't have to be." Executives with a strategic mindset surround themselves with breakthrough thinkers, or they facilitate breakthrough conversations. Here are some of my favorite techniques.

- **Make it worse.** I love this technique and share it as often as I can. It's a simple and fun break from creating a list of options on a flipchart. The facilitator poses a question to the group, such as, "How do we penetrate our untapped market in the Northwest?" Then, the team members list all the ways to *make it worse*! I.e., "don't return client calls," "avoid conferences with economic buyers," etc. Make the list as long as possible. Then, utilize the same group to "make it better" for each statement. You will discover real nuggets in the Make it Better list and have great fun doing it.

- **Creatrix® Ba.** Gather the group for silent brainstorming.

Move the team into a circle facing one another. There should be no barriers like tables or desks, just people in a circle. Write the question/challenge/aim on the flipchart in the middle of the group. With only a flipchart and marker, work for 30 to 45 minutes on solving the problem without talking. Their objective: In the 30 minutes allotted, develop at least three new ideas no one has heard of before. Again, No one can talk during this exercise.

- **Think about it differently.** Identify similarities in dissimilar objects. Give a team or teams three different objects. Each team has a different set of three objects. These can be printed on flashcards or find three dissimilar objects. Give the team or teams five minutes to list as many similarities as possible across all three objects. Ask each team to share their list. Complete a second round for another three minutes. Notice how many new ways are similar but different from the ideas identified in round one.

- **Silent mind storming.** Turn inward to solve a difficult problem by finding a quiet space, a piece of paper, and a pen. Silently brainstorm solutions to a challenge you are facing by listing 20 solutions. You may get stuck after about eight ideas, but keep going. Push your mind to deliver additional new and unique ideas. Don't stop until you have at least 20 ideas. Your last three or four ideas should be spectacular!

- **Think like a kid.** Solve the problem by thinking how a six-year-old would address the challenge. Free up the group's thinking by asking, "How would a kid solve this problem?" Let the ideas flow, and have fun!

- **Consider bold scenarios.** Assemble a small group and explore outlandish possibilities to create intriguing insights. For example, what might happen if medical science created a pill that extended life expectancy by an average of ten years, and you are a life insurance industry? How would you react? What possibilities does this create?

When using any of these techniques, notice the energy created in the conversation. Smiles, laughter, and exaggeration all ensue. And that's the point! Then, bring it back to reality. What is good or useful from our efforts? What can we run with? What possibilities exist here that need to be further explored?

Remember: you don't have to come up with the ideas; you need to facilitate idea generation.

THOSE WHO HAVE LIVED AND BREATHED AMBIGUITY

Patagonia[5], the manufacturer of premium outdoor clothing, began in 1973. Its founder, Yvon Chouinard, has spent his lifetime in environmental activism, protecting the natural world surrounding the customers interacting with Patagonia's products. He began selling hand-forged mountain climbing gear in 1957 through his first company, Chouinard Equipment. He worked alone selling his gear until 1965, when he partnered with Tom Frost, who helped him improve his products and address the growing supply and demand issues he faced.

A leader ahead of his time in achieving profits with sustainability, Chouinard first pledged to share 10% of the organization's profits with environmental conservation groups in 1985[6]. In addition to offering rugged outdoor gear for myriad sports enthusiasts, Patagonia now commits one percent of its total sales to environmental efforts, offers its own used clothing for sale on its website, proactively mitigates the risk of human trafficking in its supply chain, and connects activists with programs where they can make a difference on their home page. Imagine the pushback Chouinard faced in pressing for his sustainable practices. In 1985, few, if any, for-profit organizations undertook such a bold and consistent approach. Who would have predicted that such sustainable approaches would be profitable while considering the interests of the natural environment? Chouinard was successful despite being faced with the idea of a profitable but environmentally sustainable market awash in ambiguity.

In 2022, Chouinard transferred ownership of the company to the Patagonia Purpose Trust and the Holdfast Collective to ensure that his vision for environmental sustainability will continue to fight climate change.

Meet Tim, Chief Growth Officer for one of the largest national home builders in North America[7]. Tim feels fortunate for his career experiences. He worked for a manufacturer who captured memories across commemorative products, including yearbooks, graduation regalia, and championship rings for 19 years. During this time, he moved into new different roles every two years, from intern to CEO. He found these changes exhilarating rather than frustrating. He discovered you must adapt to each new role, and which takes curiosity and a chance to try things differently with each new opportunity.

"So often at the executive level, leaders can get become bogged down by our internal processes," Tim said. "We need to focusing externally more than internally. A key to his success is focusing solely on the customer experience by interacting with customers regularly and understanding how to make things simpler, including solutions to their challenges. While working for a powersports manufacturer, Tim found that all the exciting, and revenue-creating, features the firm had created were difficult to explain to customers on the sales floor.

He led a team that created an online vehicle configurator so customers could digitally select accessories features that intrigued them, allowing them to "see" and imagine the possibilities of their finished vehicle before purchase. This innovation positively drove sales.

Tim agreed that there is much more ambiguity in senior roles than other leadership roles. The key, he offered, is setting priorities yourself by looking at what's next for the business and for the industry, rather than being the recipient of priorities and reacting. "It's crucial for executive leaders to be cognizant, to be far enough ahead so your team can work new ideas rather than responding to them."

AMBIGUITY TO ACTION

Ambiguity, for its own sake, is not useful. Let's face it, we've all known those incredibly innovative souls. Tinkerers, dabblers, they have a thousand new ideas a minute. Yet, they struggle with converting their ideas into workable solutions. Being comfortable with ambiguity isn't about idea generation; it's about being comfortable with the information you have and making a decision given what you know. It's acting courageously, even when the outcome is uncertain, knowing that the lack of action will have a greater consequence than waiting for more information and more perspectives, in short, more clarity.

Ask yourself, under what circumstances am I most unsure? Does it happen when the outcome is uncertain or when others rely heavily on you? When you are uncertain, focus on overall intent rather than the path to get there. Work with the information you have, not the information you wish you had. Ask yourself how this might work rather than here's the problem. Consider what the worst thing that could happen is.

Yes, spend time in ambiguity, but spend only some time. Know that your knowledge and experience can be leveraged, even when you don't have a clear path to get there.

A poem about comfort with ambiguity from ChatGBT.

In shadows where the questions dance and play,
Where paths diverge, and meanings softly sway,
A heart unbound by rigid lines will find
The beauty in the chaos, unconfined.

With every twist, a new horizon calls
In whispered doubts, a deeper wisdom sprawls,
Embracing change, the soul learns how to weave
A tapestry of dreams that dare believe.

For in the murky depths, the treasures gleam
In uncertainty, we nurture hope's bright beam.
With courage as our guide, we boldly roam.
Finding our way, we make the unknown home.[8]

PUTTING IT INTO ACTION

In what ways would you like to be more **comfortable with ambiguity**?	What are you willing to **give up** on adopting this practice?

REFERENCES

1. Gelb, M. J. (1998) How to think like Leonardo da Vinci: Seven steps to genius every day. Delacorte Press

2. Byrd, J. (2013). The voice of the innovator: How the voice of the innovator can be cultivated in individuals, teams and organizations.

3. https://creatrix.com/

4. https://www.kornferry.com/capabilities/intelligence-cloud-hr-platform/korn-ferry-assess/leadership-architect

5. https://www.Patagoinia.com

6. MarcomCentral. (2024, January 18). Yvon Chouinard: How a reluctant businessman built the Patagonia brand. https://marcom.com/yvon-chouinard-how-a-reluctant-businessman-built-the-patagonia-brand/#:~:text=In%20late%202022%2C%20Chouinard%20announced,used%20to%20fight%20climate%20change.

7. Larson, T. (2024, September 20). linkedin.com/in/timlarsonli

8. ChatOn. (2024, October 28). GPT-40 (Chat GPT AI). https://chat.chaton.ai/

CHAPTER 9

Your Strategic Leaership Action Plan

And so, we are at the end of our journey and we've covered a lot. At the beginning of the book, there is no expectation that you will master all 7 mindset shifts. Through these chapters, I've explained different ways that strategic leaders can develop their thinking; some may have resonated more with you than others. Let's review.

Strategic Leadership Mindset Shifts

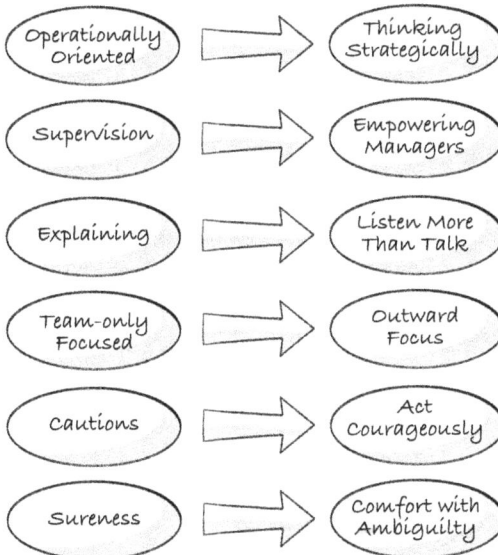

Operationally Oriented	⟹	Thinking Strategically
Supervision	⟹	Empowering Managers
Explaining	⟹	Listen More Than Talk
Team-only Focused	⟹	Outward Focus
Cautions	⟹	Act Courageously
Sureness	⟹	Comfort with Ambiguilty

Think strategically. Thinking strategically requires the leader to orient on long-term success by setting direction; and making time for "thinking" and not just "doing;" It includes moving from "here and now" to looking beyond the horizon. Acting strategically requires a holistic approach, considering broader contexts and considering market trends, competitor analysis, customer needs, and internal capabilities.

We discussed the difficulties of thinking strategically while day-to-day urgent priorities get in the way. Adopting a mindset of thinking strategically rather than tactically occurs when you schedule time for thinking rather than doing: asking more questions rather than stating your opinions; keeping abreast of industry trends and world events and understanding the impact they have on your business; and seeking international work assignments.

Empower managers. Strategic leaders must allow their managers to, in fact, manage. To do this, the strategic leader must set expectations, meet with their managers regularly, and listen to their ideas to improve the effectiveness of processes, systems, and teams. They must adopt a mindset that theirs is not the only way to get things done.

Yet, allowing managers to manage runs into potential pitfalls for the strategic leader. Developing trust with your managers before you need to rely on them is an effective strategy we discussed. Being available to answer their questions, but not taking the reins, and taking time to develop their skills before you need them are also effective strategies.

Listen more than talk. This one is difficult for many strategic leaders because they are so accustomed to leading from the front. Allowing others to freely discuss issues while being open to possibilities, demonstrating curiosity, and asking significant questions that spur insights, allows you to create listening habits that develop relationships and instill trust.

Aim to listen 70% of the time in conversations. Acknowledge others' views and expressions without applying your own judgement and incorporate a mental presence by directing your full attention to the speaker and the content of their message. Take time to build your listening skills by sitting in the silence.

Take decisive people action. Taking decisive people's action is not about avoiding a payout settlement to a departing employee. It's about your reputation. Employees notice when their boss lets bad behavior slide. Decisive people's actions do not always result in involuntary termination. Yet, these situations are uncomfortable, and we give others yet another chance. A strategic leader's mindset considers not just the individual's impact but also the impact that the individual has on the team.

Develop a mindset that sees this as an opportunity to expand the capabilities of your team while finding a better fit for your low-performing employee. Ensure clear expectations have been set with each of your direct reports, including timelines and quality expectations. Use the tools found in chapter five to identify alternate ways to resolve the situation. Your mindset can strengthen, and it takes courage to act.

Outward orientation. Managers and directors are rewarded for tactical decision-making: taking action, within the timeline and on budget. As a strategic leader, you must adopt a mindset that is outward-focused, beyond your own department or function. Such a mindset thinks about the interconnections and relationships between various elements within a complex system, a process that runs across departments, and the impact that an organization can have on their greater community and the world.

Strategic leaders do this by keeping abreast of what is occurring in the organization and supporting its initiatives, regularly attending industry conferences to keep up with global trends, taking time to develop strong networks outside of the job, and sharing their talents with other organizations, such as on boards of directors.

Act courageously. In the fast-paced and ever-changing business landscape, strategic leaders must embrace change, take calculated risks, and adjust their strategies as needed. So much is unclear in this dynamic, global economy. Having the courage to act is about valuing your intuition, leveraging the perspectives of others, acting, and then taking ownership of your decision. Courage isn't competency; it's a mindset and strategic leaders are expected to act courageously in their roles, regardless of the role they fill.

Leaders who have a mindset to act with courage will take calculated risks and step out of their comfort zone. They make hard decisions even when faced with opposition. They speak up and advocate for what is right even when others disagree, and they are highly resilient.

Lean into ambiguity. Highly effective strategic leaders who are talented at living with ambiguity have shifted their mindset by trying not to drive toward clarifying the unknowns. They understand risk, welcome creativity in solution-finding, and try ideas that may not have been successful in the past.

Being comfortable with ambiguity isn't about idea generation; it's about being comfortable with the information you possess and deciding given what you know right now. It's acting courageously, even when the outcome is uncertain, knowing that the lack of action will have a greater consequence than waiting for more information, more perspectives, and more clarity.

THE ROLE OF NEUROPLASTICITY

Neuroplasticity, also referred to as brain plasticity or neural plasticity, is the brain's capacity to reorganize and rewire itself based on experiences, learning, and environmental changes. Research in the last 20 years has uncovered that the brain is not a fixed organ but a dynamic and flexible one. It continuously adapts and forms new neural connections, strengthening pathways that are frequently used while pruning those that are not. Neuroplasticity occurs throughout a person's life, although it is most prominent during early childhood when the brain is rapidly developing.[1]

Historically, leadership was considered an innate trait, with some individuals naturally predisposed to excel in this domain; "you were a born leader." However, contemporary neuroscience research has revealed the brain's incredible ability to adapt and rewire itself. The study of neuroplasticity has revolutionized our understanding of leadership development. Rather than viewing leadership as an inherent trait, we now know that anyone can cultivate and enhance their leadership capabilities and mindsets through intentional practice and harnessing the brain's plasticity. This vast array of research has been discovered:

- Neuroplasticity shapes a leader's brain by adapting to new experiences and learning from them.

- Deliberate practice and new experiences develop neural pathways for effective leadership.

- A growth mindset coupled with a supportive environment helps expand a leader's ability and the way they think.

While seeking new experiences is a critical step to broadening one's capabilities, it also requires being in an environment that encourages trial and error and insight-building. Kennedy, Gould, and Hardie found that organizations that incorporate principles of neuroplasticity into their leadership development programs are more likely to see positive results.[2]

The brain adapts to change and reorganizes itself in response to new experiences and practice, writes Anna Tan.[3] This involves the formation of new neural connections, the strengthening of existing ones, and the weakening or elimination of unused ones. "Neuroplasticity is a constant process that occurs throughout our lives and enables us to learn new skills, adapt to our environment, and even recover from brain injuries."

Research has found that certain brain areas are linked to specific functions and behaviors. For instance, the prefrontal cortex, at the front of the brain, is involved in decision-making, problem-solving and planning. The amygdala, in the midbrain, is important for processing emotions. Tan discovered that "when individuals experience a brain injury, they can, through hard work and repeated exercise, re-channel the brain to gain some or all their mental and physical capabilities before the injury. By altering the structure and function of these brain regions through neuroplasticity, we might change our behavior and abilities."

The average human brain contains approximately 86 billion neurons, which communicate with one another through a network of 100 trillion connections, referred to as synapses. Created through a combination of genetics and experience, synapses are small gaps between neurons through which signals can be transmitted. When similar experiences are repeated, synaptic connections are strengthened. Alternatively, when synapses are not used regularly, connections can weaken or be lost completely. Therefore, when the brain encounters a certain experience or action repeatedly, the associated neural pathways are strengthened. Therefore, neuroplasticity is best activated through repetition or massed practice. The more certain task is practiced, the stronger the related neural connections become.[4]

Our brains have a vast capacity to learn and develop our thinking, even in our middle age to later years.

Dr. Irena O'Brien is a cognitive neuroscientist. After multiple years as an accountant, she followed her passion and earned a PhD in Psychology from the Université du Québec à Montréal. Conducting brain imaging and electrophysiological studies during her time there, she founded The Neuroscience School, an innovative program providing coaches and health professionals with accessible and evidence-based tools to support others in leveraging their own brain's neuroplasticity.[5] I've had the enormous pleasure of being her student.

From her research and teaching, she has concluded that developing new neuropathways requires four components:

- **A goal:** What do you want to develop? Be as specific as you can.

- **Effort:** Change doesn't occur by intention alone; a concerted effort is required that is focused on the outcome and identifies specific steps or practices to get you there.

- **Repetition:** These new connections are developed over time and through multiple practices of the same development activities.

- **Reversal:** If not practiced and sustained, the newly created neuropathways can recess to their former state.

For example, say you desire to act courageously more regularly, challenging the "elephants in the room" and moving more quickly to action. It's not enough to set the goal. You must identify strategies to develop your courage. Start small, then increase by making more courageous comments, challenging the status quo in meetings, identifying your point of view clearly, and then influencing others to support it. Adam Grant and Malcolm Gladwell have both written extensively about acting courageously. They identify two or three practices to create your new mindset. Write your ideas down clearly

THE STRATEGIC LEADER'S MINDSET

before meetings with differing points of view. Observe or read about leaders who are known for their courageousness and identify what they do differently from the way you do things. Ask a co-worker to observe your courageousness and check in with them regularly to see if they have determined a change. Review your calendar daily and identify one way you can act courageously, given the tasks or meetings you must attend.

THE ROLE HABIT-BUILDING PLAYS

Habit forming is another way to think about broadening your strategic leader mindset. Like the concepts of developing new neuro pathways, it takes time and repetition to develop new habits. Stephen Guise is the mastermind behind the concept of mini habits. He introduced the idea in his book *Mini Habits: Smaller Habits, Bigger Results*.[7] Guise suggested that by starting with tiny steps, you can create lasting habits with minimal resistance. It's all about making change so easy you can't say no.

James Garrett, a follower of Guise, has had outstanding success helping leaders adopt new behaviors with his concept of mini habits.[6] Habits, he has discovered, take roughly 66 days to form; exercise habits take longer, roughly 91 days to form.

Forming habits involves repeated behaviors that become automatic over time, like brushing your teeth each morning. New neural pathways are the physical changes in the brain that occur as you learn and practice new skills, habits, or behaviors. Essentially, habits are the routines, and neural pathways are the brain's infrastructure that supports these routines.

Forming habits takes motivation and willpower. However, while developing a habit over two to three months, our willpower may run out. 92% of us fail at our New Year's resolution every year![7]

Garret's work introduces us to a manageable strategy for developing long-term healthy and productive habits that will enable us to reach our lofty, yet achievable goals through mini-habits. Mini habits build consistency. If you do it repeatedly and over time, the habit becomes more natural.

Mini habits ensure success because they allow you to gain confidence. You exercise self-efficacy by believing in your ability to influence an outcome. Small wins build success; doing new behaviors creates confidence. I often challenge my coaching clients to set an achievable but lofty goal, such as setting up calendar time for strategic thinking, and then identify a reward when it's achieved, say, taking your spouse to a favorite restaurant.

Mini habits are small, easily achievable actions that you incorporate into your daily routine. The idea is to make the habit so tiny that it's almost impossible to fail. For example, if you want to exercise regularly, a mini habit might be to do just a few push-ups a day. The simplicity helps you build consistency over time, leading to significant change.

I recently heard a woman entrepreneur speak who started a running business to help people get into the running habit. Her secret sauce was to start small. She took members out on an initial 10-minute run. In the first few runs, they would walk one minute, run one minute, walk one minute, and run one minute. Over time, the participants increased their duration by walking two minutes, then running two minutes and so forth. This small habit-building process allowed her to create dozens of individuals who included running as something they love to do. She even groomed a few marathoners in her bunch.

Interested in mini habit building? Here are James Garrett's recommendations:

♟ Identify the habit you hope to form.

- ♟ Identify the mini habit you can incorporate into your daily routine.

- ♟ Consider tagging your new habit immediately after you do something else. For example, do ten pushups after each time you use the bathroom.

- ♟ Track your progress visibly: tick on a calendar, for example, or enter a notebook.

- ♟ Reward your new habit.

- ♟ Work on only two or three mini habits at a time.

A STRATEGIC LEADER SUCCESS STORY

I started the book with a story about an outstanding leader, Sam, who had transitioned successfully to the strategic leader role over a year. She was spending her time in different ways, delegating the "running of the business" tasks to her team, and had become a trusted advisor to the CEO.

Here's another very talented leader who has also made a successful transition. Meet Kim, vice president of sales, marketing, and customer experience for a medical packaging manufacturer. She loved her previous role as director of customer experience, and when promoted to VP a year ago, she welcomed the challenge. I asked her how she transitioned so successfully to a strategic leader.

"I'm thinking differently," she started. "It's less about doing and more about developing. I've shifted to a server leadership mindset because it's how I'm oriented. I want people to feel that they have value in our company and find joy in their work. My approach is to develop them to succeed and support them so they know that I have their back."

Kim said that to do this, she needed to establish relationships with her direct reports, working to build trust, getting to a point of vulnerability where she can have the conversations that are needed, good and bad. She also created a system that tracks their responsibilities to ensure accountability. "I delegate through a tool I discovered, and so we both know what's expected and by when."

She's added a time-blocking habit into her weekly routine. Kim discovered she needed her day to think strategically, to do the high cognitive work that she was expected to do in her role. "At first, it felt like I was being selfish. I was giving people work to do while I got to sit and think." She discovered, however, that as she moved into this new role, the CEO expected her to deliver strategically. She was required to guide where the organization was going. She needed to see the big picture and the details. So, Kim delegated more meaningful tasks to her team, which created the time she needed to engage in long-term thinking and planning.

Kim shared that she attended a seminar, facilitated by David Allen, author of *Getting Things Done*[8] who offered an easy-to-follow process for organizing and completing work, regardless of whether you are a leader in a large or small company. "He introduced me to the idea of, 'is it actionable?' was a key insight." Like every method or system, she said, you take what works for you. "This way of thinking reminds me to step back and begin with the end in mind. What is the ultimate outcome? Rather than diving into a solution, it requires me to ask myself, is this actionable and what is our outcome?"

Kim adopted this process for taking action. "Issues are messy," Kim explained. "When my staff brings issues to me, I ask them, "Is it actionable?", meaning, can we, our team or the company, actually do something about it? After discussing the issue, I then ask, "What's the next step?" or "What is the one thing you need to do?" She's found that this orientation helps keep the conversation on problem-solving, not complaining. And, she believes, she's managed the steps in a complicated issue by identifying what is next.

Kim has also scheduled "strategic thinking times." "I found that I work best in 90 minutes of uninterrupted thinking, so I create at least two blocks twice a week." To find this time, she's challenged the concept of meetings by pushing back on people who want to meet. There are many opportunities. She's discovered that a quick 15-minute conversation can resolve an issue that eight people sitting around a table for an hour can't. "It's courageous to protect your time," she concluded.[9]

I asked Kim how she manages the pop-up challenges of her role. She said she looks ahead on her calendar every week to ensure she has some open time should an urgent issue arrive. She also practices self-care. "Sometimes I need to just stand up and do a power pose. Or I just take a dance break. I have to remind myself I want to live a joyful life. Closing the door of my office and cranking up Lady Gaga and then moving, makes a tremendous difference in managing my day." She encourages everyone to take time in the middle of their day and get some fresh air, touch the grass, and reset. She reminded me it's okay to block your calendar, just ten minutes, to get outside and recharge.

She's realized over the years that she can pause and decide how she will let a situation affect her.

NOW COMES YOUR ACTION

We've discussed seven different mindsets that strategic leaders need to be highly effective at the top of their organizations.

♟ Think Strategically – Chapter 2

♟ **Empower Managers** – Chapter 3

♟ **Listen More than Talk** – Chapter 4

♟ **Take Decisive People Action** – Chapter 5

♟ **Outward Orientation** – Chapter 6

♟ **Act Courageously** – Chapter 7

♟ **Lean into Ambiguity** – Chapter 8

You've spent a couple of hours reading this book; let's make sure your time investment is not wasted. Now it's your turn to do some action planning.

Strategic Leader Action Plan	
Which strategic **mindset** would you like to tackle?	How would adopting this mindset **make a difference** in the way you lead?
What **three to five actions** will you take to begin to evolve your perspective in your selected mindset? (See the associated chapter for ideas.)	What **habits or practices** are you willing to give up to accomplish this goal?

Strategic Leader Action Plan	
How will you **keep track** of your effort?	How will you **reward yourself** when you have started regularly utilizing this mindset?

REACH YOUR STRATEGIC HEIGHTS

In a landscape where visions and strategies entwine,
a leader emerges, with purpose sublime.
Crafting a blueprint on the canvas of fate,
with foresight as a compass, they navigate.

Empower managers, let their strengths shine bright,
for in lifting others, we reach greater heights.
A tapestry woven with trust and respect,
fostering growth, where ideas connect.

Listen more than talk, for wisdom resides,
In the quiet moments where insight abides.
Every voice matters, a chorus profound,
In the dance of collaboration, true magic is found.

Take decisive people action, bold and clear,
to nurture the talent that you hold dear.
With clarity of purpose and delegation in place,
we harness our strengths, each in their own space.

In outward orientation, the world is our guide,
understanding the market, with eyes open wide.

For in every challenge, a chance to explore,
innovating pathways to open new doors.

By acting courageously, with heart and with might,
faced with uncertainty, we ignite the light.
For every risk taken, a lesson we learn,
in the fires of failure, new wisdom will earn.

Lean into ambiguity, and embrace the unknown,
for in chaos and change, a leader has grown.
With unwavering determination and a focus so clear,
we embrace the journey, prepared to persevere.

So here stands the strategic leader, with purpose and
grace, crafting the future, at a doable pace.
Through strategic insight and a heart ready to speak,
we rise as a leader, ever reaching the peak.[10]

Challenge yourself by releasing the habits and routines that have brought you to this point. Step boldly out of your comfort zone and carve out time for deep reflection. Remember, strategic thinking is a mindset—don't relinquish your power to external circumstances. Life is inherently chaotic; the true test lies in how you choose to respond. Embrace the messiness and transform it into your greatest opportunity for growth. Your journey begins with a single, courageous decision: to think differently and act with intention.

REFERENCES

1. Admin. (2024, February, 15). The role of neuroplasticity in enhancing leadership skill. Neuro Business School. https://eunbs.com/the-role-of-neuroplasticity-in-enhancing-leadership-skills/?formCode=MG0AV3.

2. Kenney, J.J., Gould, E., & Hardie, K. (2023, August 2), Becoming a natural leader through brain adaptability: How to harness neuroplasticity. Psychology Today. https://www.psychologytoday.com/us/blog/brain-reboot/202308/becoming-a-natural-leader-through-brain-adaptability?formCode=MG0AV3

3. Tan, A. (2023, February 14). Neuroplasticity and the brain science behind exceptional leadership. Forbes.com. https://www.forbes.com/councils/forbescoachescouncil/2023/02/14/neuroplasticity-and-the-brain-science-behind-exceptional-leadership/?formCode=MG0AV3.

4. Flint Rehab, Medically reviewed by Denslow, E. (2024, May 23). Can the brain heal itself? Understanding neuroplasticity after brain injury. Flintrehab.com. https://www.flintrehab.com/how-does-the-brain-repair-itself-after-a-traumatic-injury/.

5. O'Brien, I. (2024). The Neuroscience School. https://neuroscienceschool.com/about-us/

6. Guise, S. (2013). Mini Habits: Smaller Habits, Bigger Results.

7. Garret, J. (2024). How to form new habits and recalibrate your brain with James Garrett. https://www.youtube.com/watch?v=FZiN1eu6I7U

8. David A. & Fellows, J. (2015) Getting things done: The art of stress-free productivity. Penguin Books.

9. Baldwin, K. (2024, September 18). linkedin.com/in/kimberlybaldwin

10. ChatOn. (2024, October 12). *GPT-4o* (Chat GPT AI). https://chat.chaton.ai/

ACKNOWLEDGEMENT

As I said with my last book, it takes a village to create a captivating read. Here's a heartfelt thank you to my village—each of you has been crucial in bringing this book to life.

To the senior executives I've worked with over the years and those I recently interviewed, your success stories have enriched my coaching and this book. A special thanks to Kris Tucker, Bob Ehren, Rick Rittmaster, and Dan Barnes—you've shared your wisdom in each chapter, making this book better with every word.

My deepest gratitude to my husband for his unwavering support and keen editorial eye. Richard Dodson, thank you for introducing me to your vast network of book industry experts. Sue Luehring, your graphic artistry is phenomenal, and Nataliia Kokhanchyk, your illustrations breathe life into my words. Maryam Nawaz, the best line editor I've ever met, polished my prose while preserving my voice.

To everyone who pitched in with advice and support, thank you. This has been an incredible journey, and I'm proud of the book we've created together.